The BLACK GROUSE

Have you heard the blackcock's husky crow
in the cool grey light of morning,
When the mists were on the vale below,
And the mountain tops were all aglow
With ruddy gleams that seem to show
The pathway of the dawning?

Have you stooped among the heath and ling
To see the greyhen stealing
With her speckled pouts of tender wing
That closely to the covert cling
And fear to take the final spring,
Their whereabouts revealing?

Anon

The BLACK GROUSE

Written and illustrated by

Patrick Laurie

Merlin Unwin Books

First published in Great Britain by Merlin Unwin Books Ltd, 2012

ISBN 978-1-906122-43-0

Published by:
Merlin Unwin Books Ltd
Palmers House
7 Corve Street, Ludlow
Shropshire SY8 1DB, U.K.

British Library Cataloguing-in-Publication Data:
A catalogue record for this book is available from the British Library.

Designed and typeset in 12 point Caslon by Merlin Unwin.

Printed by Star Standard Industries Ltd.

Contents

Author's preface

This book shadows the progress of a single blackcock in Galloway. A region so debilitated by changing practices in agriculture, arboriculture and estate management could be seen as a poor place to study a declining species which survives only by the tips of its fingernails. This is a fair observation, but the faint embers of a failing population can be more revealing than triumphant descriptions of boom and prosperity.

I am not a scientist, and I submit my amateur observations with the excuse that natural history can never be final or definitive. It is best that I try to leave the technical minutiae of black grouse conservation to those better suited to provide it – information on the subject is abundant and very easy to come by. This book was not written to explain precisely how black grouse could be restored, but instead to show why it is so vital that we start the task today.

Patrick Laurie

Introduction

Since 1913, British black grouse have been formally described as tetrao tetrix britannicus, *a name reduced colloquially into blackgame, black, heather poult, heath poot, black heath cock, heath fowl, greyfowl and moss hen. The Gaelic language recognises them as coilleach dhubha, while they are known to Welsh speakers as grugiar ddu. For the sake of clarity, I have chosen to use the expression black grouse to denote species, and blackcock and greyhen respectively to denote sexes.*

I shot my first red grouse in the hills above Dunscore. Carrying my grandmother's twenty eight bore over the rough acres of my family's farm, a covey of five birds emerged from the closely cropped heather and my hair stood on end. They flew off to my left and I fired both barrels at the nearest straggler. A leg swung down, and after a few half-hearted wingbeats, the bird flopped into a mat of dead rushes. Being just two days shy of my fourteenth birthday, I was convinced that the shot had been quite the finest in the history of sporting shooting. I don't remember much else about the day, but my game book informs me that I also managed a running rabbit on the walk home.

As we packed the guns and stowed the dogs, my uncle, who had hosted the day, mentioned in passing that there weren't the blackcock that there used be. He had expected to have seen at least a couple. Somewhere in my head, a flicker of curiosity danced up and died again. I didn't want to spoil the day's successes by showing my ignorance, so I left the obvious question unasked. It seems amazing to me now, but at the time, I had no idea what he was talking about. As we drove the short twisted road back to our homes, I could think of nothing but my triumph.

Like many others of his generation, my grandfather lived a double life in his mid-twenties. He ran a sheep farm in the Border hills while simultaneously earning himself a reputation as one of the Battle of Britain's highest scoring spitfire aces. Known to his fellow Auxiliary Airforce pilots as 'Sheep', he moved west and bought a hill farm in Galloway in the early 1960s. True to his name, the property was used to keep blackface sheep for the next fifty years.

The Chane comprises 1600 acres of moorland, centred around a sweeping but aesthetically unremarkable ridge of just over a thousand feet in height. Seven hundred acres are covered in patchy heather to this day, while the remaining nine hundred sweep round in a vast semi-circle of whispering grasses, rushes and moss. As a small child, the moor appeared to me as an exciting and impossibly vast savannah of bog cotton and whispering grasses. Compared to my home on the Solway coast, it was wild and exotic. I spent hours sitting squarely in the moss while my family dug the peat, then I bounced and juddered in the back of a land rover all the way home to the coastal lowlands again.

On wet days, we children were watched over by the tenant farmer's wife; a smiling figure with the alchemist's ability to produce a delicious variety of scones from dull, uninteresting ingredients. For a decade, the farm existed in my imagination as a wild hill country, populated by collie pups and curlews, smelling sweetly of dry moss and rushes. When I shot my first grouse, it took on a new dimension.

After my initial success, we walked the four mile circuit around the moor each year on August the twelfth. Our bags varied. Sometimes we would hit a pair of snipe. Others, we came home with a single rabbit. Finally, my small group of young guns qualified to be allowed to shoot without adult supervision, but the absence of parents meant an absence of dogs, and we walked within inches of the birds as they crouched in the heather, flushing a tiny percentage of what was really there. We never had blank days but we came dangerously close to them, until one afternoon in 2008 when we hit gold. It had rained hard all morning but the clouds had broken up by lunchtime. The bog was wet as we walked and it exhaled under the sinking weight of each footfall. On the final 600 yard stretch back to the car, the blow grass started to crackle ahead of us. The line of six guns contracted as an ancient red grouse cock thrust his massive wattles into the sunlight.

He scolded us from a distance of thirty yards and we watched him in wonder. We were close enough to see his steel trap beak snapping with each indignant cluck. Someone to my left took a step too close and he burst into the air, cackling with premature triumph and setting his sights on the distant horizon. All around him, his brood emerged like some sort of supernatural apparition; seven birds followed his tough black figure as he purred away over the moss. Shots crackled emptily in the vast open space, and the cock and two of his young sagged into the grass with a soft bump. It was a triumph, and with the sun glancing off the Irish Sea and dazzling the hills from Edinburgh to the Isle of Man, we sat down and laughed with sheer excitement.

Over the next few hours and days, the sheen wore off our success. I began to feel guilty. It wasn't a guilt that regretted killing, but more a sense of responsibility for the birds. Each year I walked around the property, shooting one or two grouse as the opportunity arose. I did nothing for them, and yet I expected them to entertain me. The land was being used as a sheep farm, and they existed only as an accidental bonus; a relic of ancient times. After the 'big covey', I resolved to do everything I could to help the grouse, not only to boost the bag on August the twelfth, but also because I was starting to understand that country sports are based on an exchange, not an everlasting overflow of nature's bounty. Wholly ill-informed, I had vague images of burning heather and putting out medicated grit to improve grouse numbers. It was going to be a major job to encourage the birds, and within a few weeks, I had realised it.

I did have history on my side. There had been a time when grouse were one of the property's key assets. A friend allowed me to see his father's gamebooks from the 1930s, when driven grouse days were held on the neighbouring properties and triple-figure bags were not a novelty. I traced my finger down the sepia columns and felt an odd thrill to see our farm's name inked into the tables in an ornate hand. Grouse, hare and snipe were the most frequently used columns, along with one other. The word 'partridge' had been carefully ruled out above the fourth column and the letters BG had been placed above it. I asked my friend what the initials stood for and he told me.

The numbers weren't huge, but it seems like black grouse formed a noticeable addition to many walked up and driven days, not only on the Chane but also on the properties around it. Having a dozen 'BG' in the bag was not unusual for a day's shooting in 1930, but what was even more surprising was the fact that these days had been described in the 'notes' column as 'disappointing'. The author had expected even more.

At around the time that my grandfather bought the farm in the 1960s, my uncle remembered seeing as many as fifty black grouse in the hay fields behind the farm buildings. When I began my project to look after red grouse, I was under the impression that no one had seen a black grouse on the farm for at least a decade. Why that dramatic change had taken place was a total mystery to me. Having never known what I was missing, I could hardly regret it.

Most people would recognise a black grouse, but only a handful can relate more than a few basic facts about them. Nothing popularly significant has ever been written solely about black grouse, and in an attempt to avoid a weight of dry scientific data in journals, my initial research was confined to reading through books about red grouse to find the occasional relevant chapter or paragraph. Most books only gave weights, measurements and a brief sentence or two about diminishing numbers. It was only when I discovered a fresh scent from the current shepherd that my interest really began to focus.

Standing together under a crooked ash tree during a downpour in late November, we chatted about this and that while a wall-eyed collie dog blinked miserably at us from the back of her quad bike. When we came at length to talk about black grouse, I was stunned to hear that, until 2006, a bizarre black pheasant with a white puffy tail was seen strutting along a boundary fence about a mile and a half over the back of the hill. Every morning, the shepherd would take the bike around the lambs shortly after dawn, and every morning, the unusual bird would thrust its head out of the long grass and call to her. Not knowing what it was, she mentioned it to a friend who immediately identified it. The display continued for a number of years until an area of adjacent pine forest was felled and the bird disappeared without a trace.

Discovering that these mysterious grouse had been on the farm so recently was tremendously exciting. I drew up mental pictures of vast, capercaillie-like birds scooting over a line of guns through the gloom of a November twilight. These pseudo-mythological creatures occupied my thoughts for several days, but never having seen one and not knowing at all what to think of them as game birds, my imagination petered out. They were so far away from my day-to-day experience of bird life on the farm that, quite frankly, I started to doubt if the shepherd had really seen anything at all. Somewhere in the back of my mind, I doubted that black grouse even existed. After all, what were these ridiculously gaudy peacocks if not something dreamed up by the author of a science fiction novel? Moorland birds are brown and speckled, not electric blue with snowy white powder puff tails.

Over the next six weeks, black grouse slipped to the back of my mind again. It had been two years since they had been seen on the farm when I stopped in to visit the neighbouring farmer for New Year. As we talked, he grew more and more expansive on the subject of grouse and heather, and I listened in quite happily as the frost curled up against the windows and the electric heater fanned the light of an artificial flame on the walls. He remembered the days when the broken down grouse butts were still being used, and I listened to his theories of how and why the birds had vanished from his farm as well as ours. Outside, the moon blazed down on a foot of snow which had melted and refrozen into a baked surface, studded with crumbs and crusts.

He asked me if I knew about black grouse, and then told me stories of how the birds used to wander onto his hayfields by the house when he first took up his tenancy. As far as I was concerned, that was all black grouse were; nothing more than fine stories in a warm house on a frosty night. When he told me that a cock bird had been found dead having flown into a new fence just a few weeks before, I could hardly believe what I was hearing. It was a passing reference, but as I stood up to leave, and an oily coated springer spaniel came to butt its nose against my knee, I was not sure what to think. Isolated sightings here and there were beginning to paint a picture so faint and indistinct that it was hard to put it into words.

As I crunched my way home over the hill in the car, it occurred to me that if I was going to 'manage' the hill to the advantage of red grouse, I should at least know whether or not I had a population of black grouse on my hands. It meant setting out to discover once and for all whether they were on the farm or not. On paper, it was a simple task, but when you are searching a property which consists of just over two and a half square miles of thigh-high undergrowth, it is not so easy as it seems. In early March, I began to patrol the farm twice a week at dawn.

The property has a five mile boundary. I walked half of it each time I visited, so that I was sure of covering the whole once a week. Roe deer, curlews and pipits rose out of the bogs and snipe like squeaky pulleys circled high overhead, drumming and whizzing in the dark blue dawns. I walked the fences and doubled back through what I imagined were all the most likely places, but still found nothing at all. I was told that black grouse mating rituals are noisy affairs, audible from over half a mile away. At the time, I had never heard a black grouse make any sound at all and so simply knowing that I should keep an ear cocked for 'something noisy' didn't really further my cause.

Into April, I continued walking the boundary fences, stopping every two or three hundred yards and scanning around with my binoculars. I heard the first cuckoo arrive in the forest at the back of the farm and watched the skylarks hang in the air like tiny fat kites. When my father offered to take me for a look at the displaying birds in the hills between Galloway and Ayrshire, I gladly accepted. If nothing else, seeing my first 'lek' would show me what to listen for. Little did I realise that the outcome of the trip would cast a spell over me and bring black grouse to be my number one priority.

We arrived at six o' clock on a clear morning in the lambing season. I had passed the lekking site by car around a year before, but with the rising sun glancing off the hills all around, there was a different atmosphere altogether. Displaying meadow pipits parachuted out of the still air, and a velveted roe buck watched us from the verge as we turned the last corner.

My father saw them first. Fifty yards off the road, a white circle bumped and shuddered through the blow grass. I turned off the ignition and coasted to a halt as a sweet bubbling sound oozed in through the open window. Two cock birds were displaying, and every hair on my forearms was prickling. They seemed oblivious to us and to one another, bumbling through the heather like radio controlled toys. They were close enough for me to see their bloated throats shivering, bubbling with a repetitive and mesmeric rhythm. When the nearest cock stopped and stretched his neck into the sunlight, I thought that we had disturbed him. He eyed us haughtily, then jerked in a sudden spasm. Flinging his beak open, he seemed to gargle the phlegm in his throat as though he was preparing to spit, but the sudden ejaculation was not forthcoming. Instead, he bounced sharply on his toes and gargled again, striking the air with his beak as he did so. It was a display of such comic arrogance and pomposity that I could not help laughing aloud.

As soon as the first cock crowed, the other joined him, hacking up phlegm and twisting his neck as if sneezing. His wings drooped into the sparkling turf, showing clear white insignia like the shoulders of a military man. All around him, rime-encrusted blow grass crackled and hung like beige streamers. With a sudden and unexpected turn of determination, the further bird dashed towards us and his rival. Holding his head low in the grass, I could only see the very tips of his white tail as he charged. On the final approach, he rose up to his full height and more. Tottering on his toes like a spinning top and trailing his wing feathers in the dead grass, he sneezed again, wattles flaring, tail fanned out *in extremis.*

The confrontation was on, and the two birds faced one another with expressions of magnificent fury. First they pecked back and forth, then they shoved and then they thrashed against one another. Their wingbeats scuffled as the two birds fought just yards from the car. In an instant, it was over. Both had been overcome by sneezing fits, and they walked steadily apart, heads bobbing as if they could not understand what had come over them. Then one remembered. He dashed back in to fight with an expression that said 'I haven't finished with you yet, my boy!' Wattles wobbled and white underwings flashed against the creamy beige grass. A mature blackcock is scarcely bigger than a standard hen, but you would not have known it as they fought. The pompous figures looked like giants.

There is something deeply universal about watching black grouse at lek, and anyone who has got up early to see the birds displaying on an April dawn will agree that the spectacle has a wide appeal. There is an anthropomorphic humour to the behaviour, and while you may laugh to see elements of naive pomposity and silliness, there is hardly time to do so before some fresh spark of drama and violence smothers it out again. The first time I saw a lek, high up in the hills of Carrick, I watched it for an hour and a half. It had felt like five minutes. In many circles, a lek of two birds is scarcely worth acknowledging, but although I have since seen far bigger, grander leks, those two isolated birds were the start of it all. Since that morning, I have been in love.

Throughout the first days of my interest in black grouse, it never occurred to me what a massive decline they have undergone in Great Britain. There was no doubt that, as far as I was concerned, these were the most fantastic birds on the planet, but I was seeing them as an exotic species. Although I loved the lek, I might as well have been watching a pair of crested cranes in a zoo. The fact is that black grouse have not only earned themselves an important place at the heart of British natural history, but they have also forged a position in rural British culture, leading sportsmen and countrymen throughout the ages to hail them as some of the most extraordinary and iconic birds in the nation.

What was so mysterious was that I was helping to manage a farm with a history of enormous black grouse numbers, yet I was rejoicing to think that a single bird had been seen as recently as two years before. In order to see a lek, I was forced to drive forty miles through what was once one of the

Population Decline of the Black Grouse

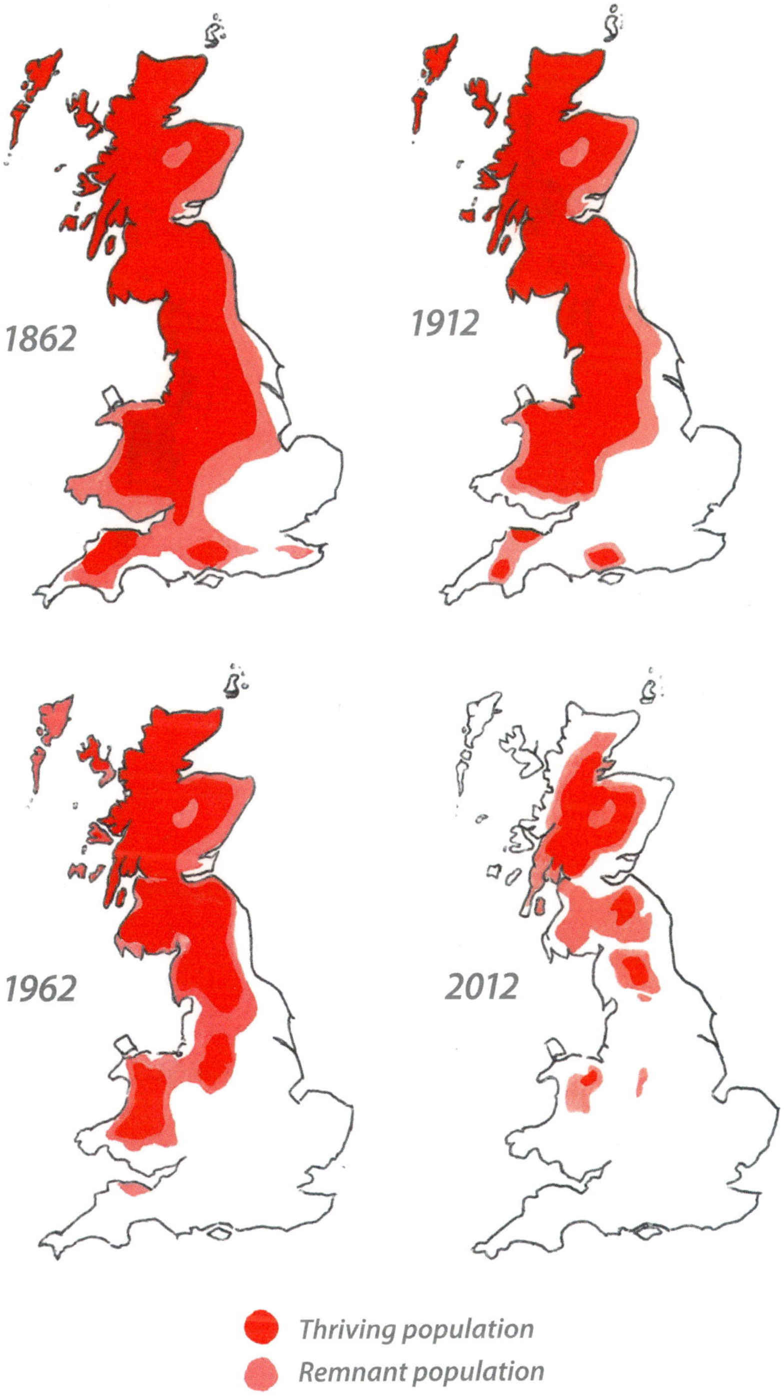

greatest black grouse strongholds in Europe. The first fact I learned about black grouse was that their range in Britain has shrunk by 95% over the past century, with 25% of that decline taking place in the past twenty five years. In Dumfries and Galloway, the disappearance of black grouse has taken place even more dramatically than in most areas, with populations falling by more than half over the past fifteen years. The sheer desperation of it amazed me. What was happening to black grouse to mean that within less than a single human generation, the birds had shifted from being an everyday occurrence to become an exotic and half-forgotten legend?

Little did I know that my 'small scale' project would soon spiral into enormity. To understand black grouse, I was forced to look back in time far further than I had anticipated. These birds have an age-old association with humans, and in order to make proper sense of where they had come from and where they are going, I had to put them in context.

PART ONE

History

A natural history of *Tetrao Tetrix Britannicus*

Thousands of years ago, the land which would one day become Britain crouched under a series of ice caps. As the climate warmed and the fragmenting glaciers crept down into the sea at last, the grated valleys and hillsides were gradually colonised by a selection of trees, animals and plants that we would today recognise as indigenous species. On the low ground, oak, hazel, alder and elm colonised the empty plains and spread into vast deciduous woodlands. Birch, Scots pine and juniper preferred the higher ground, establishing great swathes of what we now call 'ancient Caledonian forest'. Only the highest peaks and the lowest pans were free from any trees, and in the days when bears and wild cattle roamed the massive woodlands, Britain would have been an imposing place; dark, dangerous and impenetrable.

Like many other species of birds and mammals, members of the grouse family would have followed the retreating ice caps north. These were the days before Britain was an island, so an easy passage from the Continent came as standard. Grouse lived where the new trees grew sparsely enough to allow light through to the fresh undergrowth; on the verges between established forest and open ground. Wild fires and storms would have periodically ripped swathes of forest out of the ground, and the following years of succession would have been a boon for any number of plants and animals.

Our four British grouse species belong to two separate genii of the widespread *tetraonidae* (or grouse) family; the *lagopus* and the *tetrao*. There are essentially six different genii amongst the *tetraonidae*, and while almost all species within these groups are recognisably related, there are some important distinctions between them.

Taking its name from the Greek for 'hare foot', the *lagopus* genus was made famous by Britain's most celebrated gamebird, the red grouse. As the name would suggest, members of the *lagopus* genus have feathery feet which look rather like the fluffy toes of a hare, and all are adapted to live in cold climates. *Lagopus lagopus scoticus* (the red grouse) is properly a race of the European willow grouse, *lagopus lagopus*, which was isolated from continental birds after Britain became an island, taking on its own characteristics. The red grouse's closest British relative is *lagopus mutus*, the gentle and delicate ptarmigan.

The other genus of British grouse is the *tetrao*, comprising the capercaillie (*tetrao urogallus*) and the black grouse (*tetrao tetrix*). Like red grouse, British black grouse also became a distinct race following the formation of the English Channel, and seven other races have since been classified across Europe and into Russia and northern Asia. The genetic differences between races of black grouse do not manifest themselves physically, and short of blood tests, it would be very difficult to differentiate between them. Nevertheless, British black grouse are internationally recognised by the title *tetrao tetrix britannicus*, making them one of the few birds to have races which are endemic to the British Isles. There is also some evidence to suggest that the same genetic variation occurred amongst British capercaillie, but since our own race was made extinct almost three hundred years ago and the only birds in Scotland survive from an artificial influx of Scandinavian stock, it is hard to tell for certain.

Fossilised bone fragments belonging to long-forgotten members of the tetrao family have been discovered in Europe dating back in some cases more than four million years. Of all these remains, the most recognisable ancestor of the black grouse was *tetrao partium*, a bird slightly smaller than our modern *tetrao tetrix*, but physically similar in many ways. All that survives of this

ancient species is a handful of fossilised bone fragments found in Bulgaria, but scientists have been able to piece together a general impression of the bird by comparing minute shapes and measurements with modern bones.

We only have theories as to where birds like *tetrao partium* came from, but it is generally agreed that all grouse originated from a family of ancient turkeys around six million years ago. When years run into millions it is easy to lose track of what they actually mean, but if you were to imagine humans on the same evolutionary time-frame, we were still extremely hairy and primitive at a time when some fairly recognisable grouse species were taking shape.

The British black grouse needs little introduction in his modern day homelands, but it may be that for readers outside this tiny range, a brief introduction is warranted. Like many large game birds, the black grouse exhibits sexual dimorphism, meaning that the male and female birds are strongly different in appearance. An adult blackcock is a chunky, substantial bird, weighing at his largest slightly less than a moderately-sized cock pheasant. While he may be smaller and stockier than a cock pheasant, he has a very long neck which, when fully stretched, gives an inflated and misleading impression of height and stature.

The distinctive blue-black plumage attains its characteristic shimmering glossiness at around fifteen or sixteen months of age, when the last juvenile brown wing feathers are moulted out to be replaced by a uniform black from nostril to tail. The shining blue is particularly prominent on his neck and rump, and while his shoulders may carry a faint tint of brown long into adulthood, his undercarriage is always matt black. His legs are decked out in speckled grey, brown or white gaiters and his bare toes carry rows of scales which allow him to grip tightly onto tree branches and are also thought to spread his weight when walking on snow.

Many gregarious species from rabbits to geese share the classic and highly conspicuous colour combination of black and white in close proximity, and black grouse are no exception. Pure white armpits and undertails are augmented by a brilliant white 'cuff' across the wing, which unfolds to become a striking bar in flight. His immaculately contrasting sartorial appearance gives the mature blackcock a knowing air of comic pride and insolence which is unique to his species.

As a blackcock ages, his upper tail coverts curve ever more dramatically outwards. A young cock will only have a kink in his outer tail coverts, but a grand old master will show streaming tail feathers in the shape of a question mark. These feathers will flutter behind him as he flies, and his tail is so long and elaborate that he will seldom fly downwind for fear of upsetting its delicate arrangement. The classic silhouette of a blackcock's tail was traditionally compared to the shape of a lyre, but since it is nowadays harder for many to picture the shape of a lyre than the actual configuration of feathers it was traditionally compared to, it is perhaps simpler to say that they curve apart like horns of a young blackface sheep.

The pure white undertail coverts expand to form a glossy upright oval during the lek display. Sometimes, the longer feathers are tipped or flecked with black, and the random configuration of these markings can help to identify individuals, in much the same way as a fingerprint.

Above each eye, a complex comb of concentrated red tissue can be inflated

Drawn to scale, from the left: the Red Grouse, the Blackcock and the Pheasant

or totally concealed according to the occasion. At lek, the comb can be as thick as a man's thumb; by October, it will usually be tucked neatly away under a bulbous black brow line. After a morning of lekking, the thick combs subside into a garish smear of red above each eye, looking rather like the war paint of a Native American Indian.

His wings are proportionately larger than those of a pheasant, meaning that his flight is noisier, more purposeful and a great deal faster. A very distant bird might be confused with a crow or rook, but flight reveals flashing black and white underwings which leave no room for confusion. Blackcock have been estimated as being able to fly in excess of seventy miles an hour, and they would be capable of flying far faster if the birds could overcome their aversion to flying downwind for any great distance.

Unlike many ground-nesting birds, black grouse are always keen to fly and their power in the air is outstanding. Once up, they have a strong and determined sense of purpose, and this can sometimes mean that a bird will return after an extended flight to precisely the same spot where it was flushed. It often seems that a flushed bird knows precisely where it is going even before it has left the ground, and the actual flight is more of a formality than a panicked evasion. The fleeing bird can relax and look around with an expression of smug nonchalance, safe in the knowledge that escape is a foregone conclusion.

There are many occasions when it will suit a blackcock to sit tight rather than fly, and this is particularly true if he sees a dog or a fox, in which case he will clap down and only burst into flight with a sudden dramatic clatter just seconds before he is discovered. If circumstances demand a speedy escape on foot, the blackcock is quite capable of showing a fine pair of heels, and he is known for his Houdini-like ability to double back and vanish by using stealth and cunning.

By comparison, the greyhen is physically very different indeed. She is perceptibly smaller than her mate, and is barred all over with a combination of intricate colours and shades. Looking at greyhens from Scotland, England and Wales, it is fair to say that quite a wide margin of regional and genetic variety is apparent in the appearance of these birds. Some are creamy grey with chocolate brown markings, while others are rusty red and apricot. In many ways, they are very similar in appearance to hen pheasants, but with a shorter, thicker tail and a stiff, dark-coloured beak. At the risk of wandering too far from any attempt at objectivity, greyhens also have an attractive delicacy and neatness which sets them a league apart from any other game bird, male or female.

Excellent natural camouflage means that it is rare to have a close look at an adult greyhen, but the experience is often more rewarding and impressive than a passing glance at her attention-grabbing mate. A detailed inspection will reveal an unobtrusive pair of wattles which are far less outstanding than the vast inflatable sponges of a blackcock, but these combs can also rise and fall when the situation calls for it. When flushed, her wing beats are quieter than those of a blackcock or a hen pheasant, being very like the 'purring' buzz of a ptarmigan. Once on the wing, however, her flight pattern, forked tail and creamy wing stripe make her fairly distinctive, although confusion with other female game birds is very understandable. In a good wind, she can twist and turn with all the delicacy and speed of a red grouse.

The differences between a blackcock and a greyhen are more than just skin deep. At the age of around seven weeks, a male black grouse will produce the first black feathers on his neck and under his chin, and from that point

onwards, the sexes begin to diverge. Unlike the family-oriented grey partridge and red grouse, black grouse do not form coveys. Their collective noun is a 'pack', and the system of 'packing' in black grouse can be very complicated.

Young family broods break up at the end of the summer, and male poults move into one of the local packs. These packs will feed together and, when spring arrives, they will lek together, becoming almost tribal in their attitude towards territory and breeding. In modern Britain, packs of blackcock will seldom number more than thirty, and leks which reach this size tend not to expand further, with new recruits being sent away to lek elsewhere.

In rapidly expanding populations, young blackcock will often fail to win a place in a pack during their first year, lowering their chances of breeding and making them vulnerable to predation. Single cock birds may wander alone, in pairs or form new mini packs in their first year before they become strong and dominant enough to ensure a place on the lek in their second year.

This largely unstudied mechanism serves to restrict a large number of young blackcock from entering an established lek, working as a kind of pressure valve to prevent populations from becoming overbalanced by newcomers. While first year birds may become vulnerable by being forced away from their own leks, their long term survival will ensure the creation of healthy new 'satellite' leks elsewhere, which will either provide a pool of substitutes for the original lek or which will exist in their own right.

This system of controlled packing appears to be generally true today in Britain, and it is pieced together from anecdote and observation rather than any in-depth scientific study. This process is by no means a standard, and Victorian accounts exist of huge 'mega' packs which contained hundreds of birds, and leks which covered several acres. This is in keeping with several huge leks which continue to take place in Scandinavia and Russia.

Regardless of whether or not young blackcock win a place in the local pack in their first year, they will seldom stray far from their place of birth. Females are more ambitious, and greyhens will often wander many miles away from where they were raised in search of a new community of black grouse.

Large packs will always be predominated by blackcock. Many small packs will sometimes consist of a more equal balance of males and females, but it is rare for large packs to be formed exclusively of greyhens, which prefer to spend their time in a number of small groups. As the autumn progresses, larger established packs move independently around the hills, coming together with smaller groups of greyhens for seasonally available foodstuffs, but often separating again in the evening to roost.

Blackcock and greyhens have subtly different dietary requirements as the winter advances and the breeding season approaches, and the logic behind forming sex-based packs is revealed. After mating, greyhens will go off individually to scout for a nest site, while blackcock continue to display long after their purpose has been served. They play no part in raising their broods, and their packs finally break up by midsummer as the annual moult forces them to stop displaying and hide in deep cover.

The 'packing' cycle varies greatly from place to place, but it is generally true to say that blackcock and greyhens do not spend much time together, and in some cases, the lekking ground is the only place where they can be seen standing side by side.

The nearest and most direct geographical relative to the British black grouse is the capercaillie. Now that the capercaillie has all but vanished from the highlands, it is hard to study the relationship between the two in this country, but just thirty or forty years ago, the two species were frequently found to be living in close proximity. Capercaillie and black grouse occasionally interbreed, creating what is known in Scandinavia as a rackelhahn. In the wild, this hybrid is only possible after a union between a blackcock and a capercaillie hen, and only after concerted and artificial efforts under laboratory conditions has the recipe been reversed. Like other crosses between closely related species, the hybrid offspring are almost always infertile and quite interestingly, they look precisely as you would imagine them to. At lek, the cocks have the prickly throat feathers and round tail fan of the capercaillie while showing the familiar shape and wing markings of a

black grouse. Their call is a creaking burp, delivered vertically to the sky like their maternal grandfather.

It appears that when a capercaillie hen visits a black grouse lek and is mated by a blackcock, the following year will often see two or three of these mule grouse assembling, where the males will appear to fight happily with one another. However, having studied video tapes of these engagements, it is clear that they do not really understand the game they are playing, and lekking blackcock will often treat them with a cruel intolerance, scuttling away from them like spoilt bullies excluding the 'odd one out'.

Other hybrids have been recorded between black grouse and red grouse, pheasants, ptarmigan and domestic poultry, some of which stretch the imagination more than others. It became a marginal Victorian obsession to see who could collect the most extraordinary hybrids between gamebirds, and although we can now look back on many as having been wrongly identified, it is clear that black grouse can and will reproduce with a variety of different species from within and outwith the tetraonidae family.

Unlike their red cousins, black grouse will cheerfully consume an enormous variety of different vegetation. Eating everything from willow buds and pine pollen to blaeberries and oats, black grouse would appear to be the ultimate exponents of omnivorous vegetarianism. They will happily eat heather shoots, but are equally at home on a stubble field or plucking the fresh buds from the topmost branches of a young larch tree. Rowan berries slide down a treat in October and cotton grass shoots and flowers provide a welcome boost in the dark days of March. Theirs is a seasonal diet, making them seem indestructibly versatile and adaptable.

On the face of it, black grouse should litter the hillsides and red grouse should have dwindled into non-existence. The 1860 edition of the *Encyclopaedia Britannica* used this logic to present a gloomy forecast for red grouse. '*Red grouse recede where civilization progresses*', it explained, '*and they are consequently, in a fair way, at no very distant period, of being banished from England. As a vast extent of heath-land is not requisite for black grouse, there is no room to fear their extinction for some centuries to come*'. Clearly, this is not what has happened.

Red grouse are famously independent from the petty concerns of man.

They only ask to be left alone with a few sticks of heather and they show themselves to be more than capable of total independence time and time again. While it seems like evolutionary foolishness to back yourself into a corner in which you depend upon the prosperity of one plant, the relationship between grouse and heather is fruitful because no matter how fragmented and disparate heather moorland becomes, grouse will always follow it. Being much less picky in their diets, you might be excused for thinking that black grouse would be sure of tremendous prosperity.

A varied diet gives the appearance of versatility, but in reality it can make a bird deeply vulnerable. If a red grouse has a stand of regenerating heather, he is guaranteed a safe future. If a black grouse relies on an annually rotating cycle of edible materials, he is in serious trouble if even one seasonal food source is removed. Throughout the history of man's involvement with the countryside, we have shaken and wobbled the black grouse's carefully balanced system of naturally available food. In the last century, we have knocked his entire dietary calendar into chaos.

The fortunes of black grouse have inevitably become closely tied to the activities of men. However people choose to use the land around them inevitably has a direct effect on the local wildlife, but this is nothing new. Agriculture has been a changing industry for thousands of years and species have risen and fallen as human economic and social trends shifted from crofts and smallholdings to the modern 'farm'; a name which applies to a thousand different ways of using the land.

Long before man had even considered the possibility of farming in the British Isles, black grouse had happily installed themselves in and around the prehistoric woodlands. The nutritious soils of the forest floor would have supported ample quantities of rich undergrowth, and even on poor ground, heather and blaeberry would have thrived wherever sufficient light broke through to reach the earth. With muscle-bound aurochs, deer and boar roaming the forests, windblown spaces in the trees were maintained by browsers. In these clear spaces, small patches of low growing shrubby vegetation bristled invitingly upwards towards the black grouse, while at the woodland fringes, riverside meadows and bogs provided even more quality habitat.

It is hardly surprising that the climate has had an extraordinary effect on

the geography of the country. Sporadic periods of warmth and cold have swept back and forth across the hills and valleys for thousands of years, and each one has had a real and tangible impact on man's land use. Following the passing of the ice age, the forested uplands were felled and cultivated by settling farmers who made use of the warmer drier summers to plant crops. Over the course of thousands of years, these hill farms were gradually abandoned as colder and wetter weather started to prevail, making arable farming less viable in the uplands. In the absence of trees, nutrients in the soil were rinsed off the hillsides by generations of wind and rain, leaving the earth weak and poor. Heathers crept in to fill the deserted moors which once writhed and waved with cereal crops.

Today, we associate black grouse with heather moorland, but while there is no doubt that this distinctive habitat has existed in a variety of forms for thousands of years, what we see in the hills of Perthshire and the Pennines is a wholly artificial environment. Moorland only came into large-scale existence following the advent of farming and the removal of indigenous trees. Peat bogs across the nation still contain the bone-like roots of trees which were cleared centuries ago, and large areas of heather are only kept vigorous by persistent and careful burning, cutting and grazing. As a transitional plant, heather did not evolve to survive for long periods, and it expects to be overgrown by scrub and forest, occupying a brief niche to fill gaps left by fallen trees or fires. When the uplands turn purple each year, it is thanks only to sustained and costly human labour. While it is obvious that moorland formed a significant part of the original mosaic of the primeval uplands, almost all of what we today call heather moorland is manmade; clear felled, drained or farmed over the past ten thousand years.

Man farmed high on the hills during centuries of warmth, then retreated to the lowlands as the conditions changed. These tidal movements in human activity first stripped away forest, then allowed it to regenerate as an altered environment, with heathers and other shrubs having been given a real advantage. Often, the only evidence of these waves of human expansion and contraction are found in archaeological flotsam, which survives as a series of high water marks of human habitation. Dumfries and Galloway is famous for its Neolithic remains but, with only a few exceptions, the majority of ancient stone circles, cairns and field systems are now smothered in heather.

The modern observer cannot understand why burial chambers and cairns were constructed high up on hillsides, miles from civilisation, but in the distant days when these artefacts were being created, those bleak hillsides were popular human centres. They represent what Robert Louis Stevenson called the 'howes of the silent, vanished races', but they ought to be seen as waymarkers, existing to show how man has played a part in changing the nation. Alternating phases skewed the natural balance forever, inching it towards the confusing and wholly artificial patchwork that so many people today assume is natural. All the time, black grouse followed in the wake of the changes as they were being wrought on the landscape. Feeding on heather and scrubby trees throughout the year, they would have benefitted from the deforestation of the uplands and their numbers would have increased.

Centuries before the rise of sporting shooting, black grouse were being routinely killed and eaten by people across the nation. Archaeological sites like Soldier's Hole in Somerset and Gaping Gill in the Yorkshire Dales were found to contain the remains of cooked black grouse bones, and a dump at the Roman camp on Hadrian's Wall at Vindolanda had as many black grouse bones as it did the bones of domestic chickens. The birds were clearly a favourite amongst visiting Roman soldiers, and their abundance allowed them to be gathered in great numbers. History does not relate in any great detail as to how the Romans hunted black grouse, but evidence from elsewhere survives to suggest that various species of wild bird were blinded and used as decoys to snare others. Given that black grouse are strongly gregarious and that a Scandinavian hunting company still manufactures flock coated black grouse decoys, it is likely that some form of attractant, alive or artificial, was employed by the hungry Roman soldiers on Hadrian's Wall.

The ancient attitude was that wild game birds were the fat of the land and needed no bolstering. Grouse were killed on every area of upland country because the birds were there for the taking and they formed part and parcel of the daily lives of country folk. Here and there, local and tribal regulations would have controlled the killing of wild animals, but prior to the Norman Conquest, few or any laws directly applied to game birds. Following the arrival of William I, game laws were imposed by the new continental rulers, but these were largely designed to preserve deer and boar within vast and carefully policed hunting forests. The strong Norman influence spreading in Scotland in the wake of William's arrival in England saw the introduction of similar forests north of the border. However, birds were not necessarily hunted by the nobility, who preferred to pursue a more substantial quarry.

The new game laws were not only designed to prevent unauthorised people from killing deer within designated areas, but also to give those valued animals peace and freedom to procreate and multiply. While birds may not have been specifically protected, legislation to preserve the peace around deer and boar would have given a vicarious protection within forest boundaries across the nation. The New Forest was one of the first of these hunting reserves, and thanks to protection offered to deer, black grouse were able to convert the rolling hillsides of Hampshire into a major stronghold which only declined in the early years of the twentieth century.

When the monks from the great abbeys began to make way for sheep in the thirteenth century, their axes made further scars in a natural habitat that was already on the back foot. Tearing holes in the leafy eaves of the uplands allowed more and more light to hit the floor, and wild undergrowth would have leapt up to fill the gap. It was a time of great prosperity for black grouse, and it was hardly even beginning. People across the nation would have learned a great deal from the pioneering farming techniques employed by the monks, and they would quickly have seen what a difference they could

make to their environment. The practice of clear felling spread across the country. Following the Black Death, landowners realised that much of the nation's workforce had vanished and many began to experiment further with sheep, which were easier to manage and needed less supervision than the traditional systems of agriculture.

Over the course of five hundred years, hundreds of thousands of acres of woodland were cleared to encourage sheep farming and latterly in Scotland to destroy hiding places for thieves. Wherever a bog was too inaccessible to drain or improve, or where the terrain was too rough to allow trees to be felled and worked, patchy willows, birches and rowans poked through to cast shadows against the thriving undergrowth, creating interlinking pockets of ideal black grouse habitat. The trees may well have been their traditional stronghold, but the forests were being replaced by agricultural land. Around the remaining pockets of woodland lay small fields of cereal crops, hay meadows and hedge berries; food in tremendous quantities.

In the uplands, heather was grazed by livestock, and stretches of shared open moorland adjoined to inbye fields where arable land was carefully tended by farmers. A circumstance of traditional farming techniques ensured that there was enough for the people who lived on the land and plenty spare for the local wildlife, so while the trees continued to vanish, black grouse numbers became artificially inflated. In time, many regional populations of black grouse would come to depend on man's farming to complete their diets. The changes continued throughout the seventeenth century and into the eighteenth. Britain's forests were replaced with farmlands full of spilt cereals, and the poorer ground became swamped with heather, birch scrub and hawthorn.

By the start of the eighteenth century, a single unbroken population of black grouse swept from Dover to Cape Wrath, and the birds occupied a comfortable niche in more or less every county in the nation. To elaborate on an easy comparison, black grouse are in many ways our indigenous equivalent of pheasants, the two birds being dependent on similar diets throughout the year, but the black grouse being better able to deal with some native plant species and extremities of climate. In the days before pheasants arrived in Britain, black grouse performed a very similar function in the native foodchain, and appear in some areas to have been equally widespread and numerous as the

foreign pheasant is today. They could not help but make a cultural impact on the men and women who lived around them, and several aspects of their behaviour became absorbed into folk culture in an enduring way.

Stories and beliefs gradually emerged which made use of black grouse as social symbols. In some areas of the Scottish Highlands, it was considered a bad omen to hear a greyhen calling after dark. In others, the birds were seen to be unspeakably vulgar because of the supposed belief that they copulated using a weird and uncanny system of oral sex in which reproductive fluids were exchanged by spitting. Black grouse are most conspicuous at their time of breeding, and several elements of lekking behaviour were identified and absorbed into the national folk consciousness. Scottish country dancing as we know it today was essentially established following the Norman conquest, and the traditional *righle nan coilleach dhubha* [the reel of the blackcocks] is one of its lesser-known dances, in which pairs of young men bow and display to one another in a stylised imitation of birds at a lek.

The pomp and gravity of the lek led many to recognise an anthropomorphic valour and masculine prestige in displaying birds. In an attempt to harness this, black grouse wings have been worn in the caps of a variety of soldiers through the ages, and there is some evidence to suggest that medieval followers of Galloway's powerful Douglas family wore the symbol as a badge of honour. The link was extended further when men began to recognise similarities between displaying blackcock and bagpipers. Bubbling cocks periodically gasp to keep the air sacks in their throats inflated for a continuous sound in much the same way as a piper puffs into his bag, and the musical quality of the call has a similarly stirring effect as the skirl of the pipes. Blackcock became nature's bagpipers, and it did not take a great leap to transfer human values and ideas onto the birds.

Sir Walter Scott compared a black grouse lek with a competition between highland pipers in his book *A Legend of Montrose*. He writes:

> *'At length, as the black-cocks towards the end of the season, when, in the sportsman's language, they are said to flock or crowd, attracted together by the sound of each other's triumphant crow, even so did the pipers, swelling their plaids and tartans in the same triumphant manner in which the birds ruffle up their feathers, begin to approach each other within such distance as might*

give to their brethren a sample of their skill. Walking within short intervals, and eyeing each other with looks in which self-importance and defiance might be traced, they strutted, puffed and plied their screaming instruments, each playing his own favourite tune with such a din, that if an Italian musician had lain buried within ten miles of them, he must have risen from the dead to run out of hearing'.

Over many years, the link between pipers and black grouse became cemented in the Scottish national psyche, and long before the blackcock's tail became part of the official dress uniform of the King's Own Scottish Borderers, many military and civilian pipers adopted the unofficial custom of wearing black grouse feathers in their bonnets as the defining symbol of their trade. Even today, the blackcock tail is the adornment of pipers from all of the diminished pantheon of surviving Scottish regiments, although as a result of declining black grouse numbers, a variety of substitutes are available. Pipers may now wear artificially curved magpie or crow feathers in their bonnets, but the symbolic link between black grouse and military pride has proved to be an enduring one. Its martial aspects were even further embellished by the victorious British assaults on German held positions in Holland as part of Operation Blackcock in January 1945, which relied heavily on support from the 52nd (Lowland) Division; men drafted largely from the black grouse infested hills of southern Scotland.

Their stunning abundance forged them a place in the daily lives of men and women up and down the country. It was a domesticity which simultaneously respected and accessorised them. Their presence on the oat stacks during the harvest made them rather unpopular, but they were easily snared and netted to provide some variety at the dinner table. They were a tolerable pest, stealing the crops but being stolen themselves by way of compensation.

A travelling poet was amazed to visit Fort William in the early nineteenth century and watch her landlady soak barley in whisky on the washing green behind her house. Smearing the mixture on the grass, she left it for less than two hours and returned to collect a pair of blackcock, both inebriated and helpless having gobbled down the alcoholic cereals. Entertaining accounts survive of a blackcock which idly wandered into a house in the town centre of Dumfries in the early nineteenth century, much to the surprise and delight of its occupants. History does not relate what became of that bold and foolhardy bird, but it would be a fair guess to assume that it was in a pot within seconds.

Over several thousand years, man had brought about immense changes which had benefitted some species and threatened to destroy others. In England, red grouse were only surviving in any numbers thanks to heather burning and other traditional practices which also benefitted livestock. The last of the wild cattle had long faded away into history, closely followed by beavers, bears and wolves. Capercaillie passed for a brief period into non-existence, and several other species teetered on the brink of disappearance, but it was all in the name of progress. It was hard to feel bad for the vanishing species when other wild animals were making such incredible leaps and bounds. Until the mid seventeenth century, black grouse were some of the most widely distributed gamebirds in the country. They came and went as they pleased, rifling through spilt cereals and haunting the uncut field margins wherever they lay.

Cows consumed dried cereal crops during the winter, scattering undigested oats and corn across the landscape for birds to sift through at their leisure. Britain was feeding wild birds on an industrial scale, and it is no wonder that their populations boomed. Winter stubbles provided a terrific source of food, as did unguarded corn stacks and turnip crops. Black grouse could sustain high numbers throughout the year thanks to a fantastic surplus of food made available by traditional farming. They capitalised on every stage of the agricultural calendar. Despite every indication that their success was sustainable, they were on the verge of a major fall. For a brief period around the mid to late eighteenth century, black grouse rose to their absolute highest peak in both numbers and range. The next two hundred years would see them take the most tremendous and complicated plunge into obscurity, culminating today with the very real prospect of *tetrao tetrix britannicus*' extinction.

The fall seems to have coincided with the first stirrings of the industrial revolution. Across the whole of Great Britain, urban areas expanded almost overnight. The single, unbroken population of black grouse was forced to step back and fit in around the swelling cities, where humans packed themselves in like boulders in a drystone wall. As the cities grew and towns continued to expand, birds were increasingly faced with the fact that large areas of land had become hostile and uninhabitable. As a species, black grouse can deal with many problems, but they cannot tolerate isolation. Penned in and dislocated from other populations, smaller groups of birds would have quickly vanished. The industrial revolution had begun to turn land use on its head, and black grouse were amongst the first to feel the pinch. They retreated from the rolling heartlands of England to settle in areas where progress and change were less apparent.

A growing human population needed to take more than ever from the landscape, and for a bird that had become so dependent upon the perpetuation of traditional farming practices, the first significant alterations to that industry had a correspondingly massive impact on their numbers. Knox blamed the first declines of black grouse and their subsequent withdrawal from southern England in the late eighteenth and early nineteenth centuries on '*the genius of modern agriculture* [for] *enclosing wastelands and commons – where the soil, frequently sandy and poor, can never repay the first outlay of the wealthy experimentalist or the subsequent labour of his husbandman*'. A change in agricultural fashions demanded that semi-wild areas of heath or common needed to be walled or hedged, drained, worked and grazed. The knock-on effect meant that, within a single human generation, black grouse effectively vanished from southern England. It was a dramatic disappearance, and it would set the tone for the future.

JP Hamilton, a self confessed 'old sportsman' shot his first black grouse in Sussex in 1820, 'not more than five and thirty miles from London' , and another writer noted that even as late as 1939 that, within living memory, a small lek was being held on Wimbledon Common. Several other accounts exist of black grouse in a variety of places that we would today find totally extraordinary, and stragglers were being found in Norfolk, Suffolk, Surrey, Kent, Oxfordshire and Wiltshire into the first years of Queen Victoria's reign.

Despite their reduction in range, the black grouse's decline had not necessarily meant a proportionate failing in numbers. The birds were still flourishing in a massive stronghold straddling and pushing north from the Scottish Border, while healthy but increasingly isolated pockets in the West Country, Staffordshire and Wales continued to thrive. By the end of the eighteenth century, most farms in Scotland would have had black grouse for at least part of the year, and the land of the Southern Uplands was a confirmed stronghold.

Dandie Dinmont is a fictional farmer from Sir Walter Scott's 1815 novel *Guy Mannering.* A frank and cheerful sporting type, he vividly expounds the assets of his farm in Liddesdale, and with customary benevolence, he promises to take an overwhelmed youngster to his farm where he says that black grouse *'lie as thick as doos in a dookit* [doves in a dovecote]. *Ye seem tae be an honest lad', he says through mouthfuls of food. '...an' if ye'll call on me, ye shall see a blackcock, and shoot a blackcock, aye, and eat a blackcock too, man!'*

Despite their catastrophic declines in England during the late eighteenth and early nineteenth centuries, black grouse were still a force to be reckoned with. It was when wild, adventurous sportsmen like Dandie Dinmont started to look at them as something to provide sport and entertainment that their story really begins.

PART TWO

Limitation

The first attempts to pursue black grouse for sport

In his 1923 book *Amid the High Hills*, Sir Hugh Fraser describes the pleasures of stalking and game shooting in the Highlands of Scotland. He includes a description of an occasion in which a friend of his was invited to shoot black grouse in Argyll.

> *'The blackgame lived in the birch and fir woods hanging along the lower parts of the hills. Our method was to place ourselves in a break in the line of woods at the bottom of the hill, sending two or three men to drive the wood towards us. The result was usually very high birds flying downhill and very fast. On several occasions at the same time came a blackcock and a cock pheasant, of which there was a few in almost every drive. Incidentally, most of the pheasants we shot were old birds with long spurs, so were very strong on the wing. In each case - and I noticed several - the blackcock outflew the pheasant by what seemed about fifty percent, leaving him as a racing car would a 'runabout'.*

The chance comparison was very interesting, being between birds of much the same weight and size, both started under the same conditions, and I think 'doing their best'. Had the blackcock come alone, I think his much slower wingbeat would have made one think him the slower of the two.

Like many other sporting commentators, Fraser praised the speed of flying black grouse. Others remarked upon their uncanny ability to twist and turn without warning. On the whole, black grouse try to escape the dangers presented by hidden guns by moving at an unexpectedly high altitude and velocity, but when the occasion calls for it, they can turn as if on their tails and make off in another direction altogether. All accounts agree that mature black grouse (and particularly blackcock) consistently fly higher and faster than almost every other gamebird, making them a fantastic and testing quarry for sportsmen. However, in the days before shooting, these characteristics must have gone largely unnoticed.

For hundreds of years, men had hunted black grouse with nets, snares and to a lesser extent, falcons, and the first arrival of gunpowder and firearms in Britain did not change those well-established practices. All very well, the technology had arrived, but it was in such a dangerous, cumbersome and unreliable format that few people bothered to set out after flying game for many years.

The idea of shooting for pleasure scarcely existed, and guns were initially used to blast birds as they sat in trees or as they strolled along the ground. Shooting was 'pot hunting' through and through, and for decades, men expected little more from the shooting experience than an element of variety at the dinner table. Many saw firearms as a vulgar, crude method of hunting and in the light of modern fashions, it is easy to see why. Using a noisy, dangerous weapon to flatten a bird against the ground does not sound much like a real fieldsport, and in the context of traditional hunting techniques, guns were politely scorned. Nevertheless, these lethal and unreliable weapons persisted with an inexplicable popularity for centuries before they became anything like as useful and convenient as modern guns.

Since the majority of early guns (and the men who bore them) were technologically incapable of shooting birds on the wing, most game shooting involved stalking birds and shooting them where they stood. It seems that black grouse more than any other bird were traditionally shot on the ground, and the fact that they were regular visitors to cereal stubbles and arable fields meant that they were extremely accessible for the majority of country folk. Without giving the birds a sporting chance, it must have been easy for even a

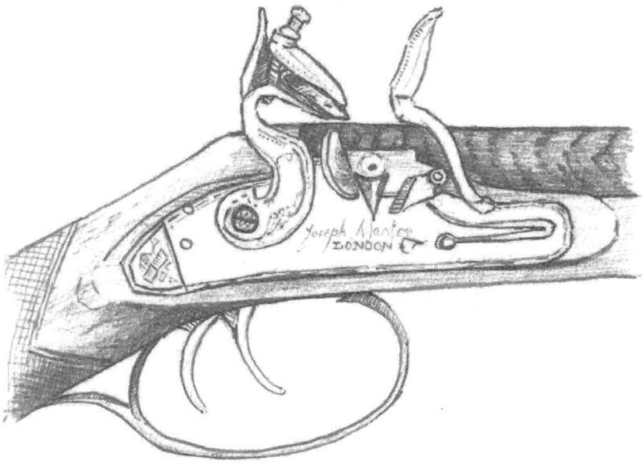

small boy to quickly gather a bag of black grouse for the dinner table, and the simplicity of black grouse hunting was plain for all to see.

The old Gaelic expression *Rhin e coilleach dubh dheth* (literally translated as 'to make a blackcock of him'), became a popular metaphor in the Highlands, carrying a similar sentiment to the modern day expression 'to make mincemeat out of him'. Perhaps the phrase originates in those days when sport was not the guiding motive for hunting, and black grouse were viewed as little more than easy meat for the first gun-toting Highlanders. The ease with which they could be killed on the ground made them a byword for vulnerability. Even in the 1930s, Duncan Campbell, the defendant in a trial held in Torridon, was quoted as having threatened to 'make blackcocks' of anyone who threatened to turn out the owners of the Ardshiels estate.

Although a date is not mentioned for the feat, Hugh Gladstone described in 1910 an occasion in which a farmer in Eskdalemuir was reputed to have killed eighteen black grouse with a single shot. Stalking a single cock bird sitting on a dyke, it had been joined by first one pack, then another, all standing in a line along the top stones. As the second pack settled in, the farmer fired his shot at about their head height, then stepped up to gather his formidable bag. Nowadays, any British sportsman would be appalled if it was suggested that he was to shoot a healthy bird as it stood before him, but this code of practice is quite new and remains relatively unique to Britain.

In mainland Europe, eighteenth and nineteenth century peasants were known to kill black grouse in tremendous numbers by using decoys and hides.

In Siberia and western Russia, elaborate cylindrical traps with swivel doors and strong nooses were used after harvests to catch birds on corn stacks where they could be promptly dispatched and consumed. Everyday folk in Latvia and Lithuania killed lekking birds by leaping out from carefully positioned blinds and clubbing them to death with sticks.

As an extension of the expression 'to make a blackcock of him', black grouse in Scotland became linked with death and vulnerability, almost in the same way as we would today associate those concepts with a 'sitting duck'. Legend has it that when the seventeenth century Gaelic bard John Lom was shown a large number of freshly killed black grouse, the hunters asked him if he had ever seen so many in one place. The bard responded that he had and more, during the battle of Inverlochy in 1645, where Montrose deceived and smashed a covenanting army far larger than his own. As a supporter of Montrose, Lom revelled in the victory, and announced that 'no harp in the

highlands would sorrow' for the death of so many covenanters, each of whom was as foolish and as easy to kill as a mere blackcock.

The mid-eighteenth century court of the Russian Empress Elizabeth I frequently took extended leave from the corridors of power to shoot black grouse as they perched in trees across the winter scrubland. These were early forms of hunting quite apart from what British people today understand as sport. The Russian gentry ensured that they had access to the best facilities, and hides appear to have been built with comfort in mind. Dotted along the roofs and perched in the trees were decoys made from black cloth, but the opulent luxury of the pastime caused some commentators to turn up their noses. A British traveller commented drily that this manner of shooting allowed the company to be '*lodged in separate parties and huts, in various parts of the woods, where there is commonly likewise good cheer; so that they enjoyed the pleasure without the fatigues of the chace [sic], with the additional advantage of society and refreshment, whilst waiting for the game*'.

While the Russian aristocracy was taking shortcuts to eliminate hardship while hunting, some early British game shooters appear to have been seeking out difficulties and hardships in order to refine and perfect new firearms technology and its application. By the mid seventeenth century, people were just starting to shoot birds on the wing, but the practicality of it was still extremely questionable. If the gunner was man enough to lug a long barrelled, heavy musket into a position from which he might be able to see a bird, he then had to contend with misfires, damp powder and scorching explosions. Each shot, whether successful or otherwise, had to be followed by the arduous and drawn-out process of reloading, which was complicated with such items as ramrods and wadding.

Despite these limitations, a few determined men rose to the challenge and fought for their sport against terrible odds. Aside from the practical disadvantages of rudimentary musketry, the wild terrain of the seventeenth and eighteenth centuries was decidedly unwelcoming. Much of the land had been cleared and worked at some point, but the rougher heaths where wild birds abounded were distinctly underdeveloped and totally inhospitable. The trees may have been cleared, but little or no thought had been given to drainage or land management.

'In earlier days', recalls Abel Chapman, 'the gunner was wont to splash ankle deep through viscous and semi fluid substances... ever running the risk of falling into unsuspected pitfalls, or finding himself suddenly embogged to the waist in sphagnum covered morasses'. Carrying a heavy gun and burdened with powder horns, wadding and shot, early moorland game shooting was more of an adventure than a sport. What little was done was carried out on an extremely small scale almost entirely by local lairds and their heartier guests. In many areas, landowners despatched their servants to shoot birds for them so that game could be enjoyed at the table without the difficulties of hunting it.

By the mid eighteenth century, the nation was undergoing an enormous change. The black grouse-infested uplands north of the border were in political turmoil, and one failed Jacobite uprising in 1715 was on the verge of spawning another in 1745. In this volatile political climate, Sir Walter Scott set Waverley, his first novel which was published in 1814. The story is a cracking yarn set before and during Bonnie Prince Charlie's return to the Highlands. As the visiting Englishman Edward Waverley is introduced to a selection of Highland worthies, he takes part in a drinking session where political allegiances are laid bare. The young laird of Balmawhapple is a coarse and robust type, with a hard drinking, straight talking attitude towards party-going. As his host starts to sing a romantic French cavalier's ballad, Balmawhapple 'broke in with what he called a d----d good song; and without wasting more time, struck up:

'It's up Glenbarchan's braes I gaed,
And o'er the bent of Killiebraid, [*bent*; moor grass]
And mony a weary cast I made
To cuittle the moorfowl's tail. [*cuittle*; pepper]

And if up a bonny blackcock should spring,
To whustle him down with a slug in his wing,
And strap him onto my lunsie string, [*lunsie*; purse]
Right seldom would I fail --'

After an ineffectual attempt to recover the second verse, he sang the first verse over again; and, in prosecution of his triumph, declared that there was more sense in that than any derry-dongs of France'. Balmawhapple's boorish behaviour upsets his host and the two nearly fall to a duel, but there is enough in his song and his bearing to illustrate the sort of hard drinking, sword wielding desperado who was prepared to walk the desolate hills for sport in the mid 1700s.

Following the failure of the 1745 rebellion, the British Government saw to it that the Highlands could never again threaten the management of the nation. Roads were enlarged, clans outlawed and lairds pressured to replace men with sheep. It was an ignominious end to a marvellously adventurous and whimsical chapter in Scotland's history, and when Sir Walter Scott began to write about adventure in the land of the Jacobite at the start of the nineteenth century, a romantically disposed European audience latched on to the idea. The threat of rebellious Jacobitism had faded with time, and the actual political insinuations of support for the Bonnie Prince had been forgotten in favour of a pleasant, rose-tinted view of doomed romance and tragedy.

Wordsworth visited Stirlingshire and the Trossachs, and an airy literary audience followed close behind him to see Scott's landscape at first-hand. These were the very first stirrings of the Scottish tourist industry, and people grew increasingly curious about the wild and misty land north of the border, even though the kilted clans had been replaced with thousands of black faced sheep, and each day dozens of Highlanders were being shipped away to America as part of the Highland clearances.

Looking back on Scotland's former remoteness, the sporting journalist James Glass wrote in 1899 of a time before Scott, where the land to the north of the border was a place unknown. 'Although moorfowl were abundant', he writes, 'none, other than those who dwelt beside them, knew their value'. It was not simple ignorance that was preventing sportsmen from recognising Scotland and the northern uplands as a sporting paradise, but a fundamental problem of logistics. Few dared head north because of unreliable and expensive transport over journeys that could well run into a duration of weeks.

One of the few early pioneers of upland game shooting encountered precisely the form of run down and shabby transport which many southerners took great pains to avoid. In 1812, Colonel Peter Hawker headed north from Carlisle in a mail coach, complaining almost as soon as he crossed the border that 'the roads and horses [in Scotland] are so bad and ill attended to, that even the mail coach gets on slowly, and in a very slovenly manner'. Hawker was a trailblazer for modern British sport, but although he could endure tremendous hardships while shooting, he was not prepared to put up with carelessness or shoddy behaviour. He later complained that 'the coachmen are a set of dirty gypsies, and the horses are fit only for dog's meat. The travelling, on an average,

I found to be about four miles per hour'. Scots did not seem to be all that interested in catering for sporting tourists, and Hawker himself was repeatedly chivvied and bothered by inn keepers and coachmen who clamoured for his money.

Nevertheless, he did succeed in getting some respectable sport, and one of his first forays after crossing the border brought him into direct contact with black grouse. On the 3rd November 1812, he wrote that 'we went out in hopes of getting a blackcock, for which this place [Moffat] has the name of being good, but after slaving till I could scarcely get one leg after the other, I found one pack, two single cocks and a grey hen, all of which were too wild to give me the least chance. Indeed, getting at them in this country (after August and September) appears impossible, as they occupy the open heights, where they generally sit like cormorants, with a sentry, either on a rock or in a tree, to give the alarm'.

The following day he had far more success after some friendly locals gave some much-needed advice.

> *'Being told that the only possible way to get black-cocks was to creep after them in the morning by daylight, I started off with my friend David Dinwiddie, and after despairing of seeing any, we espied a pack at feed; but the moment we stopped they flew up, although they were on the opposite side of an immense valley from the hill on which we were. After taking a long flight like ducks they perched on a plantation of larch firs, among some stone walls; accordingly, I began to creep when about five hundred yards from them, but having got to the end of my ambush, I found the distance too far; I then, in preference to firing at random, crept over the wall, and succeeded in getting to another, where I had a safe march to a breach within forty yards of an old cock, who was the vidette [sic] , and after crawling on all fours, with my heart in my mouth, for about one hundred yards, I gained the point, and down I knocked him, a fine old black-cock'.*

Unorthodox as they may seem, Hawker's adventures were richly enjoyed. He concluded his journey with an attempt to shoot wildfowl in the Clyde at Gourock and a few modest afternoons shooting grouse in the hills around Dumbarton, but when he returned to England the memory of the birds stayed with him. The truth is that there was a real sporting pleasure to be had in shooting black grouse, but the birds had retreated to the uplands in the early nineteenth century by the time that sporting technology allowed the public to appreciate it. Over the course of a single human generation, much of southern England had lost touch with black grouse, and while they remained aware of the birds from local folklore and anecdote, the absence of reliable transport and tourism as a popular concept meant that only the well-travelled could claim to have seen one. They still appeared here and there in rough country across the nation, but aside from huge quantities of birds in Staffordshire and the northern counties, the majority of southern English sportsmen would never have encountered black grouse.

Samuel Johnson and James Boswell's tour of the Highlands in 1773 led them around a dilapidated and financially depressed Scotland. Boswell recorded minute details in his diary, but it is interesting to note that he had a brace of black grouse shown to his friend Dr. Johnson on the Isle of Raasay because the venerable lexicographer 'had never seen that species before'. Similarly, Walter Scott's Dandie Dinmont exclaims that 'it's very odd of these English folk that come here [to Scotland], how few of them has seen a blackcock!' The range of the black grouse had shrunk back to the uplands just at the birth of shooting, but as the practice developed popularity and appeal, it reached out to touch them.

Despite the first stirrings of interest in shooting, these were still early days for moorland sport, and science was almost progressing faster than sportsmen could follow it. The advent of new shotgun actions and mechanisms allowed game to be shot 'without flint, flash or smoke', and being able to reload a light gun quickly and efficiently gave rise to the popular spread of what became known as 'shooting flying'. Colonel Peter Hawker may well have shot his blackcock as it stood on the ground before him, but he was also a quick and capable exponent of bringing birds down from the skies.

Fifty years before Hawker shot his blackcock in the hills above Moffat, a small but dedicated school of sportsmen were extolling the virtues of 'shooting flying'. Men like Scott's Balmawhapple were more than capable of bringing flying black grouse down with flintlock muskets, but that rudimentary ballistic technology was a major limiting factor. Advice to sportsmen given in 1767 appreciated the manifold difficulties of shooting flying birds, but announced with great determination that 'you must sweat and be cold, must sweat again, and be cold again, before you can arrive at any degree of perfection in this art'. However, a shortcut was not long in coming. Hawker was able to take flying birds thanks to his progressive attitude towards game shooting, and he was a fervent admirer of Joseph Manton, one of London's foremost gun makers.

Manton experimented with various new designs for shotguns and was not only one of the first London gunmakers to produce a double barrelled side by side shotgun, but he also refined existing French technologies to experiment with prototype percussion caps. In 1817, he presented a detonating double gun to Hawker which the keen shot named 'Big Joe'. Based on a new mechanism called the pellet-lock, 'Big Joe' was able to fire in any weather, and Hawker was delighted to find that he was able to shoot ducks in the rain with it. Traditional flintlocks were vulnerable to wet weather, and while pellet-locks were quickly superseded by better technologies, sporting shots suddenly had access to quality, reliable firearms which allowed them to do things that had never been possible

before. Percussion caps became the basis of the standard sporting action until the invention of the pin firing breech loaded shotgun forty years later.

Writing in 1819, technical shooting coach TB Johnson explained that, *'like most other sciences, shooting has experienced the effect of the superiority of modern knowledge; and since the application of percussion powder, has perhaps attained the acme of perfection'.* Johnson may well have been a satisfied customer, but engineering technology bent itself to improving firearms with an obsessive and competitive fervour. Leaps and bounds were made over the next seventy years to show that the detonating gun was by no means the 'acme of perfection', and it would take time for shooting traditions to catch up with the rapid progress in gunmaking technology.

Even with shorter guns which were lighter and easier to load, killing birds in the air was still a major trial for regency sportsmen. Several new guides were published to instruct and inform would-be guns about how best to go about the process. *'Shooting at sparrows is good practice, their flight much resembling that of a partridge'*, explained a booklet entitled *The Trigger*, published in 1831. *'The actual practice of shooting game is absolutely necessary in order to get the better of the trepidation and alarm which most young sportsmen feel on the rising of a covey, or even of a single bird'.*

Other guides suggested that swallows made good practice targets, but all were agreed that *'the great secret of shooting feathered game is the attainment of philosophical calmness'.* Technical limitations were still obvious. Advice published in 1836 recommended that black grouse should only be shot within a range of twenty five paces, and that with number four shot. It seems that comparatively unsophisticated shotgun technology called for close ranges and quick reactions, making black grouse an extremely testing target.

Published for the benefit of guns in lowland situations, most of these pamphlets mentioned grouse shooting only in passing. Travelling to the moors was still a wild and risky business, *'laborious in the extreme'* and testing to the patience of even the most dedicated sportsman. The scene was set for an explosion of sporting interest in Britain's uplands. Shotgun technology was advancing and a moneyed leisure class was looking for new outlets in the romantic north. In 1831, game laws were liberalised and shooting was made far more accessible.

Although the black grouse had been subject to an open and close season in Scotland since 1772 and England since the 1760s, the new laws promised to firmly enforce legislation which was being widely flouted in the remote uplands. A developing interest in game birds and an increasing ease of transport called for game preservation laws to be rigorously observed, and as James Glass recalled in the later years of Queen Victoria's reign, *'it was in 1833 that the highlands became the rage'*.

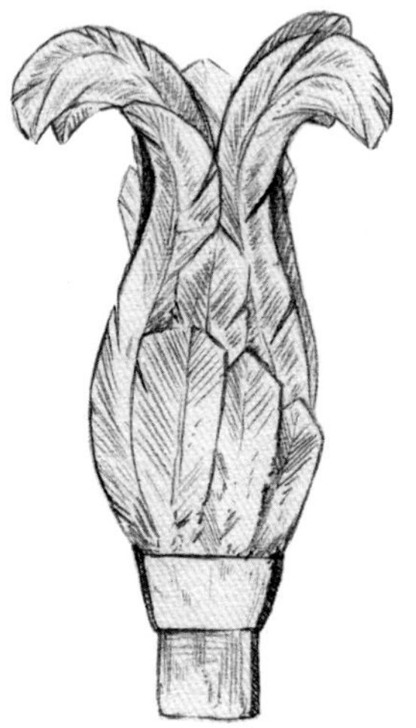

PART THREE

Progress

The advent of moorland management and game shooting

It is easy to feel a part of the natural world when you take to the high ground. In December and January, pink-footed geese struggle to clear the heather as they fly over our hill, while the summer brings wheatears and nesting teal. Cuckoos and nightjars crowd into the narrow space between the bog and the clouds. There is one road on the farm, and it runs in a half circuit around the boundary fence. Almost a thousand acres of hillside lie inaccessible to quad bikes and argocats. Quaking flows and deep, trouty streams block access to everything with an engine, so it must necessarily be explored on foot, forcing a relationship with the peat hags and the abandoned ditches. There is a timelessness to it all which is irresistible. You forget the tree roots which lurk under the peat, imagining instead that the bare, rustling acres have always been there and that they always will.

On a hot August afternoon, you can lie amongst the rushes and watch a lizard flutter his throat on a stone so covered in lichen that he is almost lost in it. Flights of newly-fledged swallows whirl overhead while voles and mice rustle the grasses with a terrified deference. A buzzing haze blurs the black hags into the bracken banks, fading away into the vast distance of the Solway flats and the mighty silhouettes of the Lake District beyond. Somewhere in the middle distance, a golden plover calls like a snoring whistle, and a soft wind wafts the smell of soaking moss over from the bog. The stillness and beauty of the uplands were some of the first and most enduring attractions of moorland shooting, and the sense of joyous isolation in the 'unspoiled' countryside provided the next step in establishing moorland gamebirds as a sought-after quarry.

In 1808, the Rev. John Vincent published a collection of shooting poems entitled *Fowling*. As you might expect from a man of God, the verses pay great attention to the glories of nature and the relationship between the hunter and his prey, but despite being couched in antiquated language and poetic inversions, the sentiments are timeless. He ignored the many challenges facing upland sportsmen in the early nineteenth century because he believed that *'the laborious toil / itself is pleasure, and rewards itself'*.

Of grouse shooting, he wrote that:

> *...No other chace*
> *Within the circling year demands such toil.*
> *With fiercest wrath the fiery orb darts forth*
> *Upon the languid frame, and ev'ry limb*
> *Is bathed with copious dews; the rugged ground*
> *With tangl'd heath o'erspread, retards the steps.*

Vincent, like Peter Hawker, was one of the first sportsmen to tackle the moors, and for him, the day was made by the *quality* of the bag, not by its weight. Reflecting in later life on his many years in the field, Hawker wrote that *'notwithstanding all* [difficulties involved in the pursuit], *I was never so much pleased with any day's sport as with my first day's blackgame shooting in England'*, during which he shot just four and a half brace somewhere on the border between Dorset and Hampshire. Likewise, as a young man in the 1820s, Charles Darwin looked forward with obsessive fervour to walking up blackcock on his uncle's estate at Maer in Staffordshire. Darwin enjoyed his sport so much that his father began to worry that the boy was becoming an idle youth, and the two men were often in conflict over their priorities.

These were the days before structured grouse shooting had begun, and the few sporting ramblers were simply happy to be away from increasingly industrialised towns and cities. It is obvious in all accounts from this period

that, even from the first days of moorland shooting, red grouse were the main quarry species of any trip to the moors, but black grouse had a major role to play in stirring up the atmosphere of variety, seclusion and natural beauty which called increasing numbers of early sportsmen back to the heather year after year. The fortunes of red and black grouse run roughly parallel for this first period of moorland shooting, although black grouse lagged behind at something of a distance from the very beginning. They were not the object of many shooting trips, but when circumstances offered a shot, it was snapped up with tremendous gusto.

An example of an unexpected sporting encounter with black grouse from early nineteenth century is given in the letters of *Rusticus*, who documented observations of natural history and sport in the neighbourhood of Godalming, in Surrey. While walking up grouse on an area of Surrey heath land, a group of three friends flushed a blackcock, who *'spread his fine curly tail, and went off like the wind. 'Mark' cried Dick, with ill-suppressed pleasure, for he made sure he had* [claimed] *his bird: but as the word left his lips, the grous [sic] threw a summerset in the air, and fell lifeless among the heather: he had received a retainer from Mr. Waring, although at a distance of more than eighty yards: a single shot, as we afterwards found, had lodged in his heart'*. Rather than bemoaning the fact that his companion had stolen his opportunity to bring down a blackcock, the gun Dick then *'threw up his hat and shouted at the top of his voice, 'Well done*

Godalming'!' Black grouse were already well on the decline in Surrey when this incident took place, and the very rarity and unexpected nature of the moment appears to have been richly savoured.

The impression from contemporary accounts seems to have been that the act of killing was merely the icing on the cake of a day in the hills, particularly if the downed bird was as fine and as memorable as a blackcock. For the older generation, it was easy to set too much importance on the death of a grouse, and many resented younger guns who were out for little more than to kill. Vincent's poem *Fowling* explains that:

> *...My soul abhors*
> *The noisy braggart, who with flippant tongue*
> *Rehearses deeds improbable*

But men of his son's generation had their sights set on a new school of thought. While conservative advice to shooting syndicates published in 1836 recommended that *'no person shall kill more than twenty brace of grouse, nor more than five brace of blackgame in any one day'*, gunmaking, ballistic technology and moorland management continued to improve. Larger bags became possible and an appetite for taking them was starting to develop, fuelled by fashion and the advent of an increasingly affluent and competitive age of sporting shooting. Within a few years, the Reverend Vincent's old school of romantic sporting rambles was ignominiously swept aside.

While individualists continued to labour alone on remote hillsides, a new species of sporting gunner looked for bigger and bigger bags. Without the cooperation of landowners, though, their demands would have been in vain. James Glass wrote that *'at first, 'shootings' were cheap enough; it came as a revelation to many 'heather lairds', as they have been called, who had all their lives, perhaps, been struggling in their endeavours to feed a few sheep and cultivate a few patches of arable ground, that there were people ready to take a lease of their lands for the sake of the moorfowl upon them'.*

As fashions developed, the 'heather lairds' realised what potential their land held and set about draining and burning the moors to the advantage of grouse. As sheep prices failed and the Australian wool market began to take control, huge tracts of British moorland started to be managed solely for visiting sportsmen. The sodden flows which had 'embogged' gunners like Abel

Chapman became crisp carpets of heather, easily accessible and overflowing with birds. With the moors increasingly populated by wealthy and fashion conscious sportsmen, excellence was demanded and received.

As shooting and hunting developed in popularity, gamebirds had started to slip ever further away from their traditional status which regarded them as belonging to the 'everyman'. Game laws were harsh and birds were becoming increasingly jealously guarded. Since the English Civil War, sporting birds had started to be gradually hemmed in and contained as the legal property of the ruling classes. By the start of the seventeenth century, the Duke of Hamilton had brought in 'preservation' laws on the Isle of Arran, the majority of which was being privately managed as an exclusive sporting reserve. When the adventurous English traveller Martin Martin wrote about the island in 1703, he noted that 'the black Cock is not allow'd to be killed here without a Licence, the Transgressors are liable to a Fine'.

Every law which bound them to the gentry gave the birds an element of prestige which they had never had before. It was still possible to kill birds anywhere, but it was only permissible as a special favour from the landlord; a privilege bestowed upon visitors and guests. Legislation passed in 1803 and 1810 'protected' black grouse in the New Forest and Somerset and Devon respectively, but these laws merely limited who could shoot the birds rather than prevented their being shot altogether. Perceptions were changing, but some were slow to adapt to the new laws.

Overnight, men and women across the country had become poachers as new legislation was brought in to make the traditional common man's right to 'pot hunt' illegal. The 1773 game laws in Scotland were widely flouted until the arrival of English sporting tenants who hated to see their leases devalued by wanton poaching. They saw to it that poachers were discovered and prosecuted, and the laws suddenly had teeth.

In many cases, 'game preservation' legislation was precisely what was needed. Despite the fact that the laws seem to endorse the unjustified sequestration of Britain's wildlife, the early nineteenth century saw a rising human population and a diminishing quantity of wild animals. Many contemporary writers from the south east of England cite unregulated hunting as being a prime cause for the decline of many bird and mammal species, and there is

no doubt that it became a major factor in the decline of black grouse. When rough ground lay near expanding suburbs and industrial centres, workers and townspeople spilled into the hills with improvised muskets and nets to take what they could. It was becoming unsustainable, and while the game laws were unpopular and morally questionable, perhaps they were justified by introducing a form of sport which could be regulated and carefully managed.

The new laws preserved game birds and gave them a legal 'owner', sparing them from potential destruction at the hands of an expanding and ravenous British population, but destroying a significant part of British folk culture without a backward glance. Many writers in the late Victorian era were prone to producing overtly sentimental pastel portraits of the people and customs of the countryside, and several rebellious poachers were immortalised as romantic heroes in the pages of these saccharine and rightly forgotten novels. One such, named simply 'the poacher' is portrayed as an eloquent rebel in *The Cottars of the Glen*, by the Rev. R. Simpson.

When reprimanded for his naughty behaviour by a village elder, the poacher explains that 'I hold that the snaring of hares, and the shooting of the wild fowls on the hill is no moral evil, for I contend that these belong to nobody. No man can lay exclusive claim to these animals and mountain birds which the gentry are now pleased to call game, and which they preserve simply for their own amusement, and I affirm that the capture of the so-called game is the indefeasible right of every man universally'. The poacher's speech almost sways a few of the cottars to his side, but the potentially tricky conflict between morality and legality is neatly solved a few paragraphs later when he slips in a ditch and accidentally shoots himself dead. His libertarian logic silenced, the cottars decide that poaching is evil and resolve to have nothing to do with it.

Despite the fact that a certain romance was developing around the poacher as a Robin Hood figure, landowners and shooting tenants were not amused. Until 1827, man traps and spring guns were still legal, and birds were preserved from poaching by pseudo-vigilante gamekeepers. Of all the birds taken by poachers, black grouse seem to have been some of the worst to suffer. Although landowners were willing to endure an element of loss in cereal crops in return for the chance to shoot one or two black grouse, their tenants were less understanding. Nests were secretly destroyed by tenant farmers looking to protect their crops, and some observers noted that collie dogs happened to have a keen 'natural' disposition towards destroying eggs. Where black grouse were not actively persecuted, many farmers turned a blind eye on poachers who sought out ways to surreptitiously pick the pests from the fields.

Advising landowners on the subject of rudimentary moorland management, William Barry gave 'one word of warning, anent the corn stooks [stacks], for it is on them that most of the poaching is carried on. Into them gather the grouse and the blackgame at the morning and afternoon feeding time, and upon them the poacher sets his wires; lying hid behind a dyke, he watches the birds flock in to feed, and as they peck the corn and are caught by the neck in the wires; they crawl, after a struggle or two, in among the corn; then out comes the poacher to secure the victims and to reset his snares'.

Numbers of black grouse were so tremendous in Sweden that birds were sold around the year at London markets, and it did not take much imagination to pass off a poached brace of Perthshire black grouse as recently-arrived Scandinavian birds. Despite high profile fears that poaching was a major factor in destroying black grouse numbers, pressure on poachers never snuffed out the black market altogether. As financial prospects developed and game laws were liberalised to allow a large demand for upland shooting, moorland birds started to become so well managed that not even illegal poaching could keep their numbers down.

Enormous quantities of birds became available to sporting tenants, and vast bags started to be taken as a result. Famously, Lord Elphinstone 'was able to fire twenty two shots, and that with one gun, before a pack of black game had passed

by'. Incidents like these represent stunning symbols of the black grouse's former prosperity as a valued gamebird, despite the fact that they are certainly nothing more than a wild dream today. There was, however, a major cost.

The moors were patrolled day and night by teams of efficient gamekeepers, and any animal which posed a threat to the wellbeing of the local population of gamebirds was destroyed. These were 'the bad old days' of gamekeeping, and some contemporary accounts make for startling and horrible reading today. Between *'1837 and 1840 on the celebrated Glengary estate, the gamekeepers destroyed the following numbers of what the keepers call 'vermin': 11 foxes; 198 wild cats; 246 marten-cats; 106 pole-cats; 301 stoats and weasels; 67 badgers; 48 otters; 78 house cats; 60 white tailed, golden and fishing eagles* [ospreys]*; 1,756 hawks, kites, falcons and buzzards, 1,913 crows, ravens, owls and magpies'.*

It was destruction on a shocking scale. Some contemporary naturalists gloomily predicted the extinction of badgers and polecats in Scotland, while others mentioned that, although foxes were by that point extremely rare in some areas, it was unlikely that these 'lucky animals' could ever be totally annihilated. It is small wonder that tremendous bags were reached when man made himself the only predator on the grouse moor.

Though the shooting of both red and black grouse was still in its early stages, both species were increasingly targeted by innovative and experimental sportsmen who were not afraid to apply techniques learned from grey partridges and pheasants in the English countryside. Shot over pointers early in the season, visiting sportsmen found that black grouse make strangely easy targets. Colquhoun wrote in 1840 that *'when your dogs point near rushes, and especially if they 'road', you may be almost sure of black-game. The old hen generally rises first, the young pack lying like stones; no birds are more easily shot... There can then be no better place to beat for them than among thick crops of bracken. Should you find them in such good cover, they will often give you a capital double shot'.*

Many experimented with walking up or pointing once the season began on August 20th, but young black grouse hatch and develop at the same pace as pheasants, and general opinion regarded shooting this early as unsporting. The

1831 Game Act had protected black grouse in Somerset, Devon and the New Forest until the first of September, but the majority of young British poults were being made legally vulnerable at a time when they could scarcely defend themselves. Latterly, shooting young birds in August was seen to be too easy, and many sportsmen avoided the practice altogether.

As Morant put it in 1875, *'it seems most unfair to commence shooting* [black grouse] *on August 20th'*. Some Victorian guns suggested putting the open season for black grouse back until mid September or the first of October, implying by their comments that they were motivated less by sentimentality and more by the simple and practical fact that it is a waste to shoot a wild bird when it is not at its best.

Ever since black grouse were given a legal season, sportsmen have argued and wrangled with one another as to the propriety of that opening date. The attitude in the first half of the nineteenth century tended towards the sympathetic, with writers commenting that *'the young* [black grouse] *are seldom full grown before the first of September; and even at this season, if they have been undisturbed previously, they will almost suffer themselves to be lifted from among the rank herbage before the pointers'*. Even 130 years later, Lord Home wrote that it *'is wrong* [to shoot black grouse in August], *for the birds are moulting and undignified without their tails, and the young ones are still unfledged. The date should be changed to mid September, by which time the birds are fair game'*. However, other forces were at work, and although moral objections were raised over the shooting of black grouse poults in August, it continued under a new guise.

As larger and larger bags became accepted as the norm, gamekeepers and estate managers began to tweak and fiddle with how the land was managed. Some theories emerged which now seem ludicrous, but which to Victorian land managers were decidedly plausible. Many estates with a great deal invested in red grouse had plenty to lose from 'ill-natured' wildlife, and keepers had a broad interpretation of the word vermin. It was written in the mid 1860s that *'the blackcock does not mix with the red species, to which it is said to be a determined enemy; so that some grouse preservers, observing that where the former increased, the latter decreased, have latterly determined to shoot the greyhens, in order to keep the stock under'*.

By the mid-nineteenth century, red grouse had started to win an ascendency in reputation and prestige over their black cousins. They were already on the way to becoming the King of Gamebirds, and it was erroneously believed that they required protection from their 'lesser' black cousins. Sportsmen felt as though they were helping the red grouse by shooting young black grouse over pointers, and thousands of greyhens and poults must have died during the early years of moorland sport at the hands of guns who believed that they were acting in the best interests of the estate.

'The birds lie very close on being first pointed', wrote *Marksman* in 1861, *'sometimes under the dog's nose, and the old greyhen is as reluctant to fly as her young; but, on being closely pressed, she suddenly rises with a startling and tremendous flutter, frightening a young sportsman to such a degree that it puts his nervous system into a great state of tremor; so that although a splendid shot offers, and a large mark, he often misses the old hen. If he can command his nerves and take a steady, deliberate shot, aiming at the head of the bird, she is sure to fall. Having killed her, let her lie at present; don't speak a word or stir a step, but load again with all possible*

dexterity, and another shot will almost immediately follow, as one or two of the brood will rise; down with them, and load again quickly as before; advance step by step, slowly and cautiously, being ready for a shot left and right; and so, one by one, the whole brood will get up at intervals, probably all within range... In this manner, every bird may be killed in the brood'.

It wasn't sport, but it was carried out for what guns believed was the greater good.

'It may look a rather cruel and harsh thing to do', wrote JD Dougall in 1865, *'but the fact is, that unless you wish to preserve black game, where the ground is unsuitable for red grouse, you cannot have both. Black-cocks are positive vermin, and will drive the more highly prized red grouse off the land'.* Oddly, his popular book *Shooting Simplified* was published with one of those damnable blackcock embossed into its green cover. Black grouse were lovely symbols of moorland and upland situations, but the very suggestion that they could threaten the prosperity of the idolised reds caused a mixed reaction amongst sporting shots. As a result, black grouse were squeezed out of a good deal of quality red grouse country by human pressure. Rather than offering variety to the moorland sportsman, they became marginalised and abandoned on the moorland fringes. A trend developed in which the best grouse moors offered red grouse and nothing else, and while the ground on all sides of the heather was littered with black grouse, few fashion conscious sportsmen had the time or inclination to pay them a visit.

In truth, recent research has shown that black grouse and red grouse have very different habitat requirements throughout the majority of the year, and it is generally incorrect to suggest that either bird attempts to 'oust' the other in a battle for moorland supremacy. Minor and isolated scuffles may well take place during the breeding season, and it may be that a greyhen seizes a promising nest site from a red grouse family now and again, but speaking in terms of national populations, direct friction between red and black grouse is of minimal concern as a cause of decline for either. Rises in black grouse numbers and falls in red could be an effect associated with habitat change or cyclical booms in parasites which suppress red grouse and have little effect on blacks, but it is incorrect to suggest that the former directly brings about the latter.

There is no doubt that, when they are at their best, black grouse offer unbeatable sport. At times, it seems as though an old black grouse has been more than a match for its human predator, and Victorian sporting literature and letters are scattered with near-misses and good-natured excuses. Even once firearm technology had been brought almost to modern standards, some blackcock still pushed it beyond its limits, flying so well as to be completely out of range for even the finest shot. Stuart Wortley described the frustrating glory of a blackcock *'turning contemptuously over your head, at the height of the cross on St Paul's Cathedral'*, and others shared his exasperated admiration. *'At maturity for sport the blackcock is a strong and cautious bird'*, wrote James Glass in 1889. *'It is well able to take care of itself, more especially after exposure for a season to the gun'*.

Victorian attitudes towards game preservation often created sporting etiquette or standard practices which were believed to benefit the stock of shootable birds. Despite the fact that black grouse lost the chance to become 'King' of gamebirds fairly early on, they did win themselves many admirers who were prepared to tolerate their presence on the stubbles and cereal stacks. In these instances, guns would only shoot male birds in the knowledge that the black grouse is a polygamous species in which the male brings no benefit to the rearing process beyond the act of copulation. The logic followed that one blackcock could service several greyhens, so the cocks were more expendable than the hens.

While blackcock were shot by the men who admired them, greyhens were increasingly rejected as a sporting bird altogether. Various sources describe the female birds as being 'thick headed', 'foolish' and 'as soft as mud', while one Victorian commentator went so far as to say that the man who kills a greyhen 'is no sportsman'. To many, their only saving grace was the fact that they produced male birds, and attempts to conserve breeding stocks meant that many estates actually banned shooting greyhens altogether. They were preserved and any gun who shot one, even by accident, was often given a firm dressing down. Like many other estates, the shoot at Oakleigh Manor, North Staffordshire, enforced a fine of two shillings for shooting a greyhen, seven shillings for shooting a second on the same day, and ten for every other after that.

As an illustration of how transient shooting traditions can be, the informal but emotive ban on shooting greyhens was quickly repealed. Landowners suddenly saw that only shooting cock birds was actively causing harm to black grouse populations. The theory was that leaving too many infertile old greyhens around for the breeding season is disruptive and prevents fertile birds from sitting. There has been little evidence to prove that greyhens do become barren in later life, but for whatever reason, shooting female birds has clearly been shown to improve black grouse stocks in a number of instances. It is clear that whatever the reasons behind the selective shooting of sexes, the general sentiment of sporting guns was well meant.

While some young guns and misguided factors massacred juvenile birds in August, many others did not. They remembered gripping encounters with full grown birds later in the year and knew that the best was yet to come. But they couldn't wait forever. Social calendars only really allowed guns a few

weeks in the hills before partridges and, later, pheasants came in in England. Delaying the shooting of black grouse meant that as the autumn drew on and partridges began to beckon in England, many tenants and their guests began to think of heading southwards. The awkward delay meant most guns had left the hills by the time that black grouse could be properly shot.

John Colquhoun's advice to would-be game shooters in 1840 explained that *'as the season advances, black-game are the wildest of all birds. Fair open shooting at them is quite out of the question...'* Sporting journalists uniformly mention a change which takes place over the course of a few weeks when a switch seems to flick in the heads of young black grouse and they turn from being the easiest birds to shoot to become by far the hardest. The young blackcock had a small window of sporting potential, sometime between mid September and mid October, and enthusiastic sportsmen racked their brains to invent new ways of exploiting the birds' natural habits. Their wariness made them impossible to point with dogs after late September or early October, and as Peter Hawker had found, difficult stalks were the only real way to have any success after those weeks. As an aside, in the absence of shooting, most modern black grouse are often surprisingly tame, and many of the remarks made by Victorian sportsmen who studied birds closely during the shooting season have become irrelevant to today's birds.

Other variations for shooting black grouse emerged, such as 'pop' drives or ambushes, but it soon emerged that, although they were thoroughly enjoyed, none really satisfied the developing criteria for fashionable sport. The practice of firing at feeding birds from the window of a cart, or of using a horse and cart as a diversion while birds could be stalked emerged in the Scottish Borders as a way of shooting reasonable numbers of black grouse, but subsequent portrayals of this practice in sporting literature did not do much for the reputation of the birds.

We are told that *'on approaching blackcocks with a cart, they are all visibly on the alert, with necks up on full stretch, and evidently unable to comprehend the raison d'etre of the phenomenon. It may of course only be a harmless farm cart, but if ever they commence so to grapple with the problem, their distrust and suspicion invariably overcome their reasoning powers, and they take to the wing at three or four gunshots distance'.*

Colquhoun offered another possibility for dealing with exasperatingly wild birds late in the season, but it too was loaded with drawbacks. '*Your best plan*', he wrote, '*is to hide yourself among the sheaves* [of corn], *and wait for their feeding-hours. If you are well concealed, and select the proper part of the field, you may have an opportunity of killing a brace sitting with your first barrel, and another bird with your second*'. John Walsh also mentioned this practice in 1856, but he seems to have had far less patience for it. '*It is tiresome work*', he explained, '*and not worthy to be called grouse shooting*'.

Personal tastes aside, shooting black grouse was a minefield of problems in the traditional sporting calendar. The comparative ease of walking up red grouse or shooting good numbers of them over dogs had started to edge the smaller birds ahead in the popularity stakes. Sportsmen became used to shooting at coveys of red grouse, and they were often frustrated by the black grouse's refusal to form cohesive and shootable groups. When August the twentieth arrived, they found greyhens with their unsporting broods on the low ground, and moulting blackcock scattered here and there throughout the heather. The season for walked up shooting drew to a close by the time that black grouse came together to form packs, which, unlike coveys, are often vast, unpredictable and constantly alert to any danger. Launching an assault on a pack of black grouse was quite different to walking up families of red grouse, and it involved an entirely different system of strategy and know-how. When a new practice emerged in the mid nineteenth century involving beaters and rudimentary butts, upland shooting would change forever.

The stunning escalation in game bag numbers in the mid nineteenth century has its roots in the appearance of driving as a shooting technique. It is unclear as to precisely where grouse driving emerged, although several have claimed the credit for having invented it. It is probable that it existed in an unexploited form for decades before it took off as a fashionable pursuit, and accounts survive of driven grouse shooting in its most basic form taking place in the early years of the nineteenth century.

Dr. Walsh gave it a brief description in 1856, explaining that '*when grouse become very wild, two modes are sometimes adopted of getting shots, which are pursued chiefly in the most hilly moors. The first consists of driving, by means of the gillies, the grouse over or within shot of certain spots where the shooters are concealed.*

In those moors where walls are met with, one of these places of concealment is selected, and the sportsmen kneel down behind, at intervals of sixty yards from one another, and in such likely situations as it is supposed the grouse will fly over, when disturbed on the opposite hill... This is sometimes, towards the end of the season, the only mode of filling the bag, but it is a tedious kind of sport, and more befitting the keepers than their masters'.

Beforehand, early exponents of 'shooting flying' had been warned that *'when the bird flies in the shooter's face, as it were, or towards him, he should let it pass before he attempts to fire, or he will be almost certain to miss'.* Sportsmen were not up to shooting birds passing overhead, partly because of the basic level of firearm technology, and most preferred to walk up their birds and shoot them from behind. The advent of driven shooting as we would recognise it today was made possible by demands for big bags and tremendous leaps in gunmaking. By the time that pin firing breech loader shotguns came on the market, rapid firing and reloading had become the defining characteristic of game shooting. The new guns allowed driving to claim precedent as the cream of moorland shooting, sealing the eternal glory of the red grouse. Increasingly seen to be seasonally awkward, uncooperative and elusive, black grouse had already started to spin a downward spiral.

PART FOUR

Non-Conformists

Black grouse come in second best to their red cousins

The largest bag of black grouse ever taken in Scotland came from Glenwharrie, a system of farms and moors in the extreme north of Dumfries and Galloway. On the fourth of October 1869, a team of eleven guns shot 247 head. The list of guns included H.R.H. Prince Christian of Schleswig-Holstein, Count Hompesch, Viscount Masham, the then Duke of Buccleugh, three Lords, two Lieutenant Colonels and a man simply named as Edward Balfour. The names are now almost meaningless today, but the titles tell a story of their own. This had not been an idle day's walked up shooting across the farm.

Nine years previously, the largest ever British bag of 252 birds had been shot on Cannock Chase in Staffordshire, and across the black grouse's range, triple figure days were becoming less and less surprising. No longer were either grouse species treated as a fortunate by-product of agricultural industry; they had become a valuable asset in their own right.

The new craze of driving red grouse also encompassed black grouse and swept them along with it, turning them into a major target for Victorian sportsmen. On some days, like that at Glenwharrie, the shoot had been clearly engineered towards them. The total bag was 247 black grouse (200 cocks and

47 hens), 40 hares, 21 partridges, five red grouse, two rabbits and one pheasant, and the participation of Prince Christian had brought the black grouse to be a gamebird by Royal Appointment.

It was only when transport and mobility reached out to touch the upper classes that modern upland sporting shooting came into existence. In 1859, 'the Paddy Line' opened up the southwest with regular services running from Carlisle to Stranraer, preceded a decade before by express railway lines up the east and west coasts to Edinburgh. Vast tracts of formerly inaccessible grouse country from the Southern Uplands to the Outer Hebrides was opened up for exploration within the space of a decade, and sporting tourists flooded into the wild moors of the North.

Writing in the early 1860s, HG Adams included a section of verse which illustrates the booming sporting industry which, though still in its embryonic stages, was already drawing hundreds of English guns north of the border each season.

Oh come! For the heather has purpled the hills,
The crags are all golden, and bright are the rills;
And far o'er moorland the call of the bird
By the ear of the sportsman delighted is heard.
The greyhen has led forth her fledglings to feed,
Till they're heavy and plump and are prizes indeed;

... Yes, come to mountain and come to the moor;
We sound not the pibroch, nor draw the claymore:
The sons of the mist to the Saxon give hail,
And welcome them all to the land of the Gael'

Queen Victoria's acquisition of the Balmoral Estate added an extra pull for socially conscious sportsmen, and word quickly travelled that a fashionable and apparently inexhaustible sporting heaven was sitting directly on England's doorstep. Whereas before, Colonel Hawker had taken days to reach Scotland, Londoners could step onto a sleeper at King's Cross and reach the moors by morning. Grouse were a major attraction for sporting shooters, and as soon as their habits and preferences became widely understood, they started to be shot in fantastic numbers, driven towards the butts by teams of beaters.

It sometimes happened that black grouse and red grouse flew together off the same stretches of heather, and these moments were admired by some for their variety and excitement, but when specific attempts to drive black grouse were being discussed, it was in reference to something very different.

Commentators throughout the mid to late Victorian period remarked on the 'magnificent sport' offered by shooting driven blackcock, and some land (mainly in the south of Scotland) began to be managed with quality black grouse days in mind. However, despite improved technology, the 'high class sport of driving fully feathered black cocks in late autumn' still carried with it a distinct flavour of earlier and more rudimentary shooting.

Looking back on a life in the shooting field in 1937, Lord Scott attempted to explain his early fixation with shooting driven black grouse, providing a brief example of the sport on offer.

> *'A pack of these magnificent birds is seen feeding, probably on a hillside stubble, or even on the bare hillside. The guns crawl along and are placed along as sheltered a line as is possible across the general line of flight, which the keeper should, of course, have previously observed. When flushed, the black-cocks come over in a black mass, if down-wind, at an appalling speed, sometimes very high... making an almost terrifying spectacle. This is a really high trial for the nerves, for we only, at best, get a few shots, but if we miss it is like being bowled out at cricket, for we don't get another chance until the second innings'*

It was not easy to drive black grouse, and there were many strict rules which needed to be followed if any chance of success was to be met with. Scott continued by observing that

> *'it is essential with blackgame to keep out of sight when moving to one's shelter, and where there is a large pack, no shot should be fired before the driven cocks on the wing are nearly up to the guns. On a particular occasion, a huge pack of about a hundred and fifty cocks was located on a stubble. It was desired to drive them into some natural wood up a small glen. If once manipulated into this, they could be driven back again with a considerable chance of a satisfactory toll being taken from them. The host warned his guests on no account to fire before at least one of these cocks had crossed the wall behind which the guns were hidden. In spite of this one man fired at a pigeon which happened to rise sixty yards in front of him. The pack rose in one black mass, flew in a body into the blue. As it was the afternoon, there was no chance of getting hold of the blackcocks again, and a good afternoon's sport was lost by one absurd shot'.*

It was a risky business, filled with difficulty and chance, but there is no doubt that guns of the old school would have approved. This was true sporting shooting, and some guns forsook the ever-expanding driven red grouse days to take their chances and crawl into position around the feeding packs of blackcock. In some drives, the guns were banned from smoking and talking in case they disturbed the feeding packs. On others, entire local families were turned out to distract birds, block stubbles and push small and wary groups together until the 'big flush' by a system of gentle beating.

The practice of driving depended on a great deal of daily reconnaissance by gamekeepers. Black grouse will fly on recognised flight lines, but these will change if the birds are intercepted too often. The sport was sporadic and unpredictable, requiring a combination of walked up shooting, stalking and military style organisation. There were enough practitioners to keep it trundling along as a respected (and in some areas very lucrative) branch of moorland shooting, but general consensus increasingly viewed it as being decidedly inferior to driven red grouse.

This sense of inferiority arose steadily and would slowly extinguish black grouse as a gamebird. Interestingly, it had nothing to do with the birds themselves. The sportsman's increasing disinclination to shoot black grouse and to focus his attentions on red had its roots entirely in human fashions, and both species of grouse looked on indifferently as guns extrapolated on the numerous merits and demerits of the various techniques used to shoot them.

As Walsh explained in 1851, when driving grouse first emerged as an accepted practice, it existed to fill the bag towards the end of the season, after the more prestigious practice of shooting over dogs had taken precedent. As years went by and red grouse became more and more abundant, moor owners started to realise that not only did driving from the twelfth make financial sense, but that it also helped to keep increasingly enormous grouse stocks healthy by thinning out older birds and scattering coveys. The more that driving took place, the more men learned from doing it and the better and more efficient they became at it. A practice that had begun in England crept northwards until it reached the stage at which it took precedent over all other types of moorland shooting.

The once respected technique of shooting over dogs was quickly rejected in favour of driving, which not only allowed for more luxury and relaxation, but which also boosted bag numbers to startling new heights. During the brief transitional period from dogs to driving, lovers of grouse were sharply divided on the subject of which practice was the purer. Reminiscing on a long life in the field in his 1928 book *Retrospect*, Abel Chapman recalled the disputes which took place during the mid nineteenth century between those who preferred to walk up their own grouse and those who chose to have them driven. It is obvious which side he favoured.

'Grouse shooting was once largely a sort of one man pursuit in the wilderness', he wrote. *'Today it is rather transformed into a social function - a brief transference of Mayfair into the moorland'*.

The craze for driven grouse was starting to become solely guided by finance and fashion. Tenants rejected the traditions of driving and chose to start shooting red grouse from the butts as soon as the season began, demanding excellence from day one. With big bags at a premium, estate owners had a great deal to lose by running a disappointing day.

Grouse driving is based upon the practiced belief that, when carefully flushed from cover, red grouse have a tendency to fly a similar route to safety. As a result, permanent drystone grouse butts stand on hillsides from Cornwall to Caithness, used throughout generations to intercept the whirring coveys, year after year. A day's red grouse shooting guaranteed that if the birds on the moor could be correctly driven, they were certain to present some form of shooting for the waiting guns.

Correctly marshalled and flushed, red grouse are always sure to provide sport. Breeding successes and the weather conditions on the day will always make a difference to the numbers available for shooting, but if there are birds on the moor, they will always fly in the same direction. Black grouse are decidedly less predictable, particularly when they are still with their young and are keeping to the lower ground early in the season. If they are present on the moor at all during the last fortnight in August, they are wary and skittish. They will be approaching the end of their moult and the blackcock will not have their long tails or characteristic glossy blue-black feathers. They will use a number of different routes to escape from a beating line, potentially slipping past the guns or doubling back over the beaters to waste time for serious sportsmen who were out to set up a tally. Many guns watched blackcock wheeling high overhead, well out of range, returning to land where they had been flushed after a brief circuit of the moor. Some mistook the distant shapes for ducks, misled by long necks and high altitude flight paths.

Attempts to turn black grouse towards the guns by using flankers with brightly coloured flags failed as the determined birds seemed to fix on some point in the distant horizon, then headed towards it, high and fast with an unshakeable resolve. In some instances, the appearance of black grouse rising from the heather with a noisy clatter would panic the reds, causing both species to fly at a tangent away from the guns. Where black grouse were seen to be taking red grouse out of a drive, they began to earn themselves a reputation

for being a bit of nuisance. If the occasional blackcock did fly with red grouse over the butts, he was a bonus. If he didn't, he risked harming the success of the drive. Black grouse were so unpredictable that many hosts may well have been reluctant to experiment with driving moorland known for strong black grouse populations for fear of disaster and disgrace.

Figures from gamebooks throughout the golden years of grouse shooting in the late nineteenth and early twentieth century may well show inordinately high numbers of black grouse killed, but these figures seldom match the numbers of red grouse in the bag at the end of the day. It may be that it was less common for black grouse to fly over the butts than reds early in the season, or that they lacked that magical and manic cackle. It may even be that they were harder to hit, but either way, black grouse were always second best, not only in their contributions to the bag, but also in their cultural importance. Perhaps red grouse have such an aura of excitement and adventure that anything else would pale by comparison. The fact that black grouse often made up almost half the bag on thousands of driven days was inconsequential because it was only 'almost'. One hundred red grouse and ninety nine black was still a red grouse day, and that was what the fashionable guns were paying for.

Red grouse have a famous and well-established link to heather. Small inter-linking territories cater for their every need, and barring severe weather, once a breeding pair has raised a brood, they will continue to haunt the same few acres of heather. By comparison, black grouse do not occupy territories in the same way. They are more than capable of travelling miles to feed, seeking out seasonal foodstuffs as the year revolves. They might pass the winter in a stand of mixed deciduous woodland with access to heather moorland, then move several miles to lower, boggier ground throughout the spring and summer. As a result, a black grouse's seasonal transience made them harder to care for and less reliable to find when the shooting parties arrived.

It was noted as early as 1834 that *'there is no such thing as keeping* [black grouse] *at home: all the Dukes in Christendom and all their keepers could not do it'.* In response to this capricious behaviour, moorland management was always going to be geared towards red grouse, who were easier to find and protect than blacks. The sedentary behaviour of red grouse made them 'money in the bank' for estate owners, while black grouse were uncooperative wild cards.

While the butts were loaded with the wealthiest and most influential men of the day, the great traditions of shooting grouse over pointers continued to chug along in the background, greatly diminished in followers and popularity. Chapman grumbled about the new and decadent fashions which scorned his old ways, but some of his remarks are very interesting when they come to dealing with shot game.

With the pained self pity of the persecuted, he wrote that *'all those who did not at once embrace the new 'cult'* [of driven grouse] *were contemptuously classified as 'pot hunters'.* With the elaboration of sport as fashion, guns were losing touch with the traditions of country sports. Driven grouse shooting had become less about using skill and fieldcraft to outwit a quarry and more about the social and technical side of racking up a big tally. Bags were symbols of opulence, and while dead birds were gladly sold or distributed by game dealers to the fashionable gastronomes of London, the link between numerical figures and actual quantities had become something of an irrelevance to the men and women who had shot them. In theory, it would take a team of eight guns a little over four months to comfortably eat a thousand birds, but these numbers started to be reached day after day.

It is not irresponsible to shoot more than you personally can eat, but the sheer scale of the bags was starting to drive a wedge between traditional practices and changing fashions. Estates made good money selling the birds to game dealers, and many guns sent crates of grouse to friends in the south as a kind of fashionable calling card. Mrs. Beeton's *Dictionary of Everyday Cookery* pays some attention to black and red grouse, noting that the blacks held more than double the value of their smaller cousins in 1865, but mentioning in passing that a good housekeeper should not buy game from a game dealer at all. It is inferred that a fashionable household would have the birds sent to them from the moors by a friendly sportsman, sidestepping the vulgarity of everyday commerce. As far as black grouse are concerned, Mrs. Beeton advised her readers to *'reserve the thigh, which is considered a great delicacy, for the most honoured guests, some of whom may also esteem the brains of this bird'*.

Shot birds were clearly not wasted, but good sport was now measured solely in numbers. Those who rejected the new criteria and chose instead to try experimental driven days at black grouse were seen as second class sportsmen, even though their attitudes towards sporting shooting was a quality over quantity approach that can easily be sympathised with today.

Writing in the late nineteenth century, the black grouse enthusiast Charles St John reflected on how bag numbers had become so much the primary concern that there was a genuine pressure to conform to the new fashions. He explained that he had *'much more satisfaction in killing a moderate quantity of birds in a wide and varied range of hill... to the disgust of the keeper, who may think his dignity compromised by attending a sportsman who returns with less than fifty brace'*. There is no right or wrong approach to game shooting, but at a time when red grouse were earning their title as 'The King of Gamebirds', social pressures were clearly at work to depress the reputation of the tricky and unpredictable black grouse.

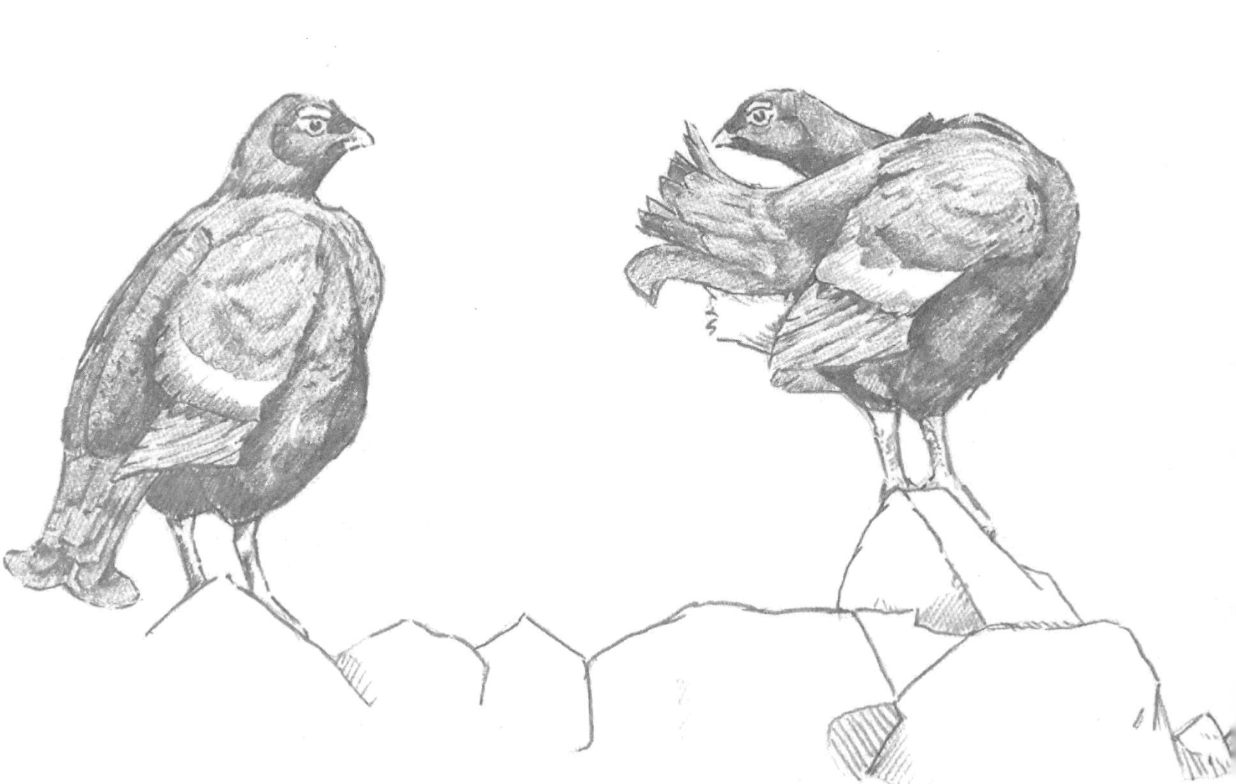

The informality and apparent scruffiness of driven black grouse offered a wholly different experience to the close packed excitement of driven red grouse, and was always destined to remain the slightly 'down at heel' cousin. After all, Lord Scott had *crawled* into position behind a drystone dyke. Many exponents of driven red grouse had spent too much money on bespoke shooting suits to be seen crawling through the mud in them. They preferred to be driven to their butts, have the birds driven to them, then be themselves driven away again.

As driven black grouse started to become known as slightly downmarket, the birds themselves were quickly relegated to the sidelines. With the rise of driven shooting, game shot using risky and improvised methods became 'birds for the pot', symptomatic of traditional subsistence and rustic domesticity. Walked up, stalked or improvisationally driven birds retained an unpalatable aura of labour and hard work, and once driven shooting had taken hold, general consensus slammed the practice as wearisome and distastefully hearty.

Black grouse belonged to a sporting world where sweat was a virtue. They came into their own once the high society golden days of August had passed. The wealthy men who could afford to maintain grouse moors throughout the year for a few weeks of sport early in the season cared little about a bird that

was not really available as a quarry species during that time, and to some extent, they drifted back again into their old status as the farmer's bird.

In Scotland, so much of what had been done to improve moorland for grouse had been carried out by English sportsmen, few of whom had the spare time to stay north of the border for a chance at an unpredictable quarry when pheasants loomed large at home. In a way, black grouse became the property of the locals; shot by keepers to keep numbers down and flighted as pests by farmers and tenants. There is evidence to suggest that while in many areas poaching red grouse was a cardinal sin, poaching black grouse was seen more as an irritating inevitability.

Conflicting attempts to suppress black grouse in favour of reds and encourage black grouse stocks for shooting were often chronologically simultaneous. In some areas, black grouse were pests to red grouse stocks while in others they were valued and admired. On the big red grouse moors, keepers discouraged black grouse from mixing with the reds, forcing them away from the heather. Unwelcome on the moors in many places, black grouse found a suitable new home amongst upland farms and bogs alongside grey partridges and hares. They had been shut out in the cold, making their new strongholds away from the grouse moors.

While red grouse numbers soared and the King of Gamebirds was being crowned by sportsmen across the world, black grouse had become parochial, rustic and awkward. They played a large part in the day-to-day lives of men and women in the uplands, but while lekking birds were admired as beautiful symbols of moorland nature, they were increasingly seen as background noise by sporting tenants, many of whom described them as 'sundries' or 'various' in their game books, along with rabbits, pigeons and rooks. Sportsmen may well have had any number of fantastic Archibald Thorburn prints of black grouse on their walls, but when it came to the crunch, most would always prefer to shoot at red grouse.

Black grouse refused to conform to the new fashions without a fight. They thwarted human fashions and alienated themselves from a sporting community which demanded to be able to stand by and have birds come to them. Fashionable guns would only encounter a handful of blackcock during the first few weeks of the driven season, then would have returned to the lowlands for pheasants by the time that Lord Scott's 'magnificent sport' became possible by mid October.

It was tricky to drive them. The period during which it was possible to point them was short and occupied an awkward few weeks in the game shooter's social calendar. The practice was starting to become mildly scorned. Eclipsed by the predictability and atmospheric genius of red grouse, blacks had slipped into the difficult middle ground between shooting styles. They couldn't be labelled. Single guns idled away a day pursuing them with traditional techniques here and there, and landowners might invite a friend for an afternoon's driven shooting where an anomaly in the terrain might force black grouse into a reliably shootable circumstance. But as a fashionable gamebird, they were fading away.

Some guns continued to use traditional techniques to shoot blackcock on the ground, but advancing fashions had little patience for these old and rustic ways. Despite recommendations published in Scotland which described stalking blackcock as 'very exciting sport', the practice was scorned by the leading lights of sporting fashion. Even into the twentieth century, a young John Buchan could be found creeping around the dykes of Tweedsmuir for a chance at a standing blackcock, but social pressures eroded the practice more and more over the years. It became an idle boy's sport, or a rude farmer's diversion, and with the total decay of stalking, 'shooting flying' had closed the door on its traditional forbear. In a similar timescale, the once popular practice of stalking and shooting wild geese with rifles faded away as the shooting community cut off and rejected traditional practices which they viewed as 'unsporting'. In terms of fashion, the shooting press vocalised a widespread belief that black grouse were 'a disappointment' and 'of little interest to the minds of many shooting men'.

Despite the fact that black and red grouse generally have very little to do with one another and neither feel any great animosity towards the other, the belief that blacks kept down reds was one that took a great deal of time to die away. It was still being acted on in the late 1960s, when a land rover was dispatched from a well-known grouse moor in the southern uplands to collect shooting volunteers from Dumfries. Free cartridges were handed out, and the men were allowed loose on thousands of acres of hillside in the Dumfriesshire uplands with instructions to shoot all black grouse on sight. There must have been tremendous sport on those subsidised days, and it was not uncommon for six guns to return home with more than fifty black grouse in the bag. The only benefits from this antiquated attempt to boost red grouse numbers were felt by the volunteer guns. As long as the estate considered black grouse as pests, men were free to enjoy shooting that would have been the envy of their fathers and grandfathers.

From the late nineteenth century onwards, it was almost as if black grouse were assuming the verminous cloak currently worn by the woodpigeon, which in itself is a finer sporting target than any pheasant ever bred. Both black grouse and woodpigeons fly strongly and present unique sporting opportunities, but because they refused to be driven in huge numbers, they became somehow ostracised and neglected by the trendsetters of the shooting community. Thanks to decoys and specialised fieldcraft techniques, the woodpigeon now has an army of sporting admirers. If a sudden downturn in woodpigeon numbers suddenly took place, farmers would rejoice, but I have no doubt that their dedicated army of shooting friends would see to it that steps were taken to stem it.

Black grouse never won a sufficient number of those valuable human friends who shot them and nothing else, so their disappearance signalled the removal of a single column in the rough shooter's gamebook, rather than the destruction of an entire branch of sporting shooting. Tony Jackson's 1974 book *So you want to go Shooting* pays them only a short reference, mentioning that '*it is unusual for blackgame to be the particular object of a foray; they are more usually encountered in a grouse or capercaillie drive, when they will often cross the line at considerable height*'. Regardless of how they flew, black grouse had largely ceased to exist as an independent quarry species.

Shooting has changed immeasurably. On the whole, the obsession with bag numbers has found its way into the history books, and that can only be a good thing. A sport that has greed and excess at its heart is an unhealthy and unsustainable practice. Ideally, a true sportsman defines a good day by being able to remember each bird he shot, equally rueing each he missed. He ends a season with a list of memories based not on quantity but quality.

Many guns from the late Victorian and Edwardian period have left detailed gamebooks to show how sporting bags have changed. Look through a few of these dusty books and you will soon grow tired of numbers stacked upon numbers. They are dull and say little about the individual experiences which drew sportsmen north year after year. Your eye begins to stray to the 'comments' column; single sentences or paragraphs about specific incidents which took place during the day.

More often than not amongst moorland guns, the comments columns recall brushes with black grouse - extraordinary moments which last far longer in the memory than any series of numbers. Exclamation marks and underlined words used to describe unexpected and magical moments carry through the generations to show that the same things that would excite us, thrilled them all those years ago. An enduring pleasure of Victorian sporting shooting was the much underrated element of surprise and variety. Mixed days of walked up shooting may not have allowed any game species to become the 'star of the show', but with the prospect of a black grouse always lurking around the corner, they came as close to any as representing the true spirit of Victorian rough shooting.

Without exception, the guns who had the patience to pursue black grouse by stalking or improvisation write warmly and respectfully about their experiences. After all, a second's excitement with an unexpected quarry is at the heart of country sports and remains far longer in the memory than any number of big bag days. It would be hard to come up with a better accolade than that published in the *Shooting Times* 1963 guide to grouse shooting, which states that *'there is no more exhilarating bird at which to shoot than a full feathered black cock when he comes at you at head height like a driven grouse, or like a pheasant well up in the air and at high speed'.*

PART FIVE

Decline

The historical root of habitat collapse

I had been searching the Chane for black grouse for six weeks, and was continually drawing blanks. The circuit around the farm was growing longer and longer with each fruitless lap. I was on the verge of forgetting the entire operation. If there were black grouse on the farm, they were so scarce that it would be pointless trying to help them. I had started to drive up to the hill as much to scout for roe deer as look for lekking birds.

One dull blue morning towards the end of April, I drove up to the farm and left dark fingerprints in the condensation on the galvanised gate as I closed it behind me. It promised to be a bright day, but a thin mist still hung on the stones at the top of the moor. A curlew whimpered conversationally in the rushes below the road, and I swung the car up the hillside to the right, sweeping the silvery wet grass into a dark green passage. Two hundred yards up the slope, I turned and parked my battered 1996 Vauxhall Astra where the rushes began to grow thickly. As the engine stumbled into silence, a deliberate song flooded through the open window. It was ten to five, and I wasn't sure if I was dreaming or not.

Two hundred yards away, a neat white oval was wobbling in the rushes. Grabbing for my binoculars, I focused them as quickly as my sleepy fingers would allow. The song drew to a sudden conclusion. As if from some heavenly void, I heard a rasping, spittle-soaked sneeze. The rushes fuzzed in the binoculars, and then I saw him; an adult blackcock performing a tidy lek on an area of recently mowed rushes above the shepherd's cottage.

Excitement, satisfaction and sheer relief flooded over me in equal measures as I watched him patrol his tiny corner of the field. His wingtips trailed in the dew and his shiny throat bristled with feathers like a goatee beard. After five minutes, he stopped lekking altogether and hunched moodily into the long grass. He preened his wings and stamped his feet, then glared sulkily at me through the morning light. I would have been less surprised if he had said 'good morning'.

All my searches through the wet bogs at first light on the furthest reaches of the farm seemed like a pathetic waste of time. I had found precisely what I was looking for just forty yards away from the farm buildings. Looking at the indistinct black shape through the steamed lenses of my cheap binoculars, my mind raced with questions. Was he lekking for a greyhen? Was he lekking with another blackcock that I couldn't see? How could I keep him here? Why had he just appeared after an absence of two years?

The most stunning and seemingly unanswerable question was where had he come from? I now know that, judging from his brown wings and incomplete tail fan that he must have been less than a year old when he arrived, so where was his family? It was as if he had simply fallen from the sky. A lekking cock bird presents such an extraordinarily exotic spectacle that I even began to wonder if I had made some sort of a mistake and was actually looking at an escaped parrot.

I can now guess that forestry operations on an adjacent area of land probably pushed him off the lek site where he had started his annual displays, but the sheer unexpected nature of his arrival beggared belief at the time. An ambitious and commendably successful attempt to keeper grouse on a neighbouring property has since shown a steadily rising number of black grouse, and it could even be that this bird was one of theirs, cut off or dislocated somehow from his home range.

In many places, black grouse appear to have vanished altogether over the past ten years, but this is not always the case. It is easy to imagine that if the birds are still around, they would be hard to miss, but in many cases, when

black grouse fall below a certain number, they become invisible. Very small populations are easily overlooked altogether, particularly by shepherds and farmers who are distracted by looking over stock. In an environment where there is a very small scattering of birds, the only evidence of black grouse will be found by a tremendous amount of silent and patient observation. In many cases, lone cock birds in isolated situations seem to lek secretively in thick cover, so an observer who expects to find the barefaced arrogance of a displaying blackcock in plain view can sometimes be disappointed.

This secrecy is sometimes attributable to good sense, particularly in scattered populations where birds do not have the security of numbers which they evolved to rely upon. I witnessed a blackcock's nail-biting escape from a goshawk who ambushed him while he was lekking alone on open ground early one morning. Following the attack, the blackcock drew an abrupt halt to his conspicuous displays and for the next month, he would only lek under cover of total darkness, between ten o'clock and two in the morning. He spent his days crouching silently in thick cover, but his nocturnal displays still drew in at least one greyhen, who raised a single poult to adulthood. In the absence of a large pack of comrades, lone or isolated birds are forced to innovate, particularly in their strategies for avoiding predators. As a result, their behaviour can deviate from the 'classic' norms in so many ways that it's no wonder that they slip past unnoticed in many areas.

Over the next few months, I started to see signs of other birds across the farm which could only have been there all along. I found unexpected feathers and saw dull shapes in the distance, all of which contributed to a vague and incomplete picture of a horribly diminished population of birds. It was amazing that, given the Chane's history, they were still wandering around our hill.

The First World War is often cited as having been a watershed for the British countryside. Before the conflict, millions of men and women lived and worked on the land. More than 20,000 gamekeepers stalked the hedgerows and moors of the nation, and each one strived to destroy every predator on his given beat. After the treaty of Versailles, less than one third of that number returned to their former employment. Thousands had been killed in front line fighting, and landowners could no longer afford to employ surviving staff on a scale comparable to the pre-war years. The changes took some time to take effect, but when they did, they were tremendous.

Although black grouse bags taken from the vast Drumlanrig estate remained relatively stable during the first three years of the Great War, averaging at three and a half thousand birds a year, they fell by more than a half over the next seventeen years. Foxes had been so heavily persecuted that they had become a rare sight in many upland areas. Crows, weasels and stoats had dwindled into obscurity along with some species of raptor, but as the people of the countryside struggled to come to terms with the enormity of the war's tragedy, the vermin began to stage a slow recovery.

The traditional upland estate had run groups of small, independently tenanted farms with a vested interest in game shooting. Many landowners had been reduced to ruin by the war, and these vast yet tightly bound clusters began to disintegrate as farms started to be sold away in packages or as independent items. Changes in farming practices throughout the nineteenth and twentieth century saw the absolute demise of the small upland farm. The associated changes to habitat quickly manifested themselves. Poor quality land needs a great deal of work to make it profitable, and as small crofters and tenants moved away or were ejected from the countryside, a tendency towards ranch farming developed, where the boundaries between multiple smallholdings were demolished so that several farms could be run together as one large repository for livestock.

The new 'ranch' farms were too large to manage in the traditional ways, but too small to employ a gamekeeper. Even existing and well established estates began to suffer as they sold off the surrounding land and found that some new owners did not control their vermin, and foxes and crows drifted over from neighbouring properties.

Ranch farms no longer needed to be self-sufficient entities, since feed for the animals could be grown on better land elsewhere and brought in. Valuable winter stubble fields and cereal stooks had traditionally formed a key element of the black grouse's seasonal diet, and their populations collapsed as the number of independently operating farms fell through the floor.

In the days when sporting landlords shot their farms, tenants came under some pressure to forgo some of their harvests so that there would be a shootable population of wild birds. Black grouse flocked like rooks onto the unprotected stacks, and while it made little agricultural sense to waste large volumes of valuable cereal on black grouse, Victorian sportsmen lurked around the fields in a state of tremendous excitement. After the First World War, the upland farms which continued to grow cereals were run by individual farmers who could not afford to lose large quantities of corn to benefit the birds, and since many were no longer answerable to sport-oriented bosses, black grouse were treated as agricultural pests. What seems so surprising today is the fact that it was a status that they deserved.

Even in the 1950s and early 1960s, a farmer in the uplands could spend a morning flighting black grouse into his cereal stacks and consider that defence of his crops as work. The birds had started to be habitually destroyed by honest men and women who had genuine fears for their livelihoods. Some early twentieth century sporting guides recommended that, in order to curry favour with the local farmers, the visiting grouse shooter should take a day off from 'real sport' to offer his services to protect the oat stooks from black grouse. Increasingly, the implication of this suggestion was that the favour was more for the farmer than for the sportsman.

The former tenants had little interest in burning areas of heather 'on rotation' as before. They burned away huge swathes to allow better grazing for livestock, destroying old heather which red and black grouse use to nest safely. Fresh heather growth was quickly nibbled off by sheep, and overgrazing stripped back and destroyed birch and willow scrub. 'Ranch' farms began to appear across not only the Southern Uplands but north into the Western Highlands and south into Yorkshire, Lancashire and Staffordshire. Operating a large area of poor ground needed a tremendous investment to keep it viable. In due course, drainage and basic maintenance was neglected and the agricultural value of the un-worked land fell drastically.

Lord Home relates an incident which took place on a driven shoot during the early years of the twentieth century where King Edward VII had invited a Russian Count to shoot with him in the hills of the Scottish Borders. The Count was more used to shooting bears than birds, so he was placed at the end of a line of butts for the sake of safety. Home explains that '*during the drive, pack after pack of black game flew past him and he never fired his gun. Asked by the King the reason for his restraint, he replied, "I thought they were the poultry from the farm over there"*'. It was an entertaining moment, but it not only illustrates the fact that black grouse had come to exist in great numbers around farms and worked fields, but also suggests that an implied agricultural domesticity had contributed to make them second class gamebirds.

Black grouse had become so linked to and dependent upon farming practices that they were increasingly cast in an unfortunate light. They had developed a commonplace agricultural familiarity which bred contempt. It was a link that would go on to have disastrous effects for the birds.

As a final body blow to the sporting potential of upland farms, the Second World War brought about a nationwide paranoia about the provision of food.

Hitler came so close to starving the nation to death that the post war years were a time of obsessive agricultural productivity. Numbers of sheep across the southern uplands crept higher and higher in response to a fear of starvation that had seemed very real while the U-boats had stalked the North Atlantic. Eventually, overgrazing stripped much of the traditional heather from the hillsides and left open pasture. In addition, stacks of marl and lime were brought in to scatter on the acidic soil to make it more productive for sweet grasses. 'Improved' pastures like these have little nutritional value for any wildlife and have been improved only in an agricultural sense. Since 1945, Scotland alone has lost a quarter of its heather coverage due to over-grazing and commercial tree-planting.

In more recent years, the unreliable value of livestock meant that the maintenance of these newly-cleared fields was neglected, reducing them into savannas of wet ground, tufted by rough grasses and soaking in moss. Nature reclaims agricultural land very quickly in the uplands. Stone walls collapsed and arable fields became incorporated into pasture over the course of just a few years. By the 1990s in Dumfries and Galloway, hayfields had started to become a rare sight on hill farms. Blow grasses and sedges choked out the remaining heather and wallowed in the wetness of broken drains and burns that no longer knew which way to flow.

Many landowners abandoned farming altogether and sold their land to the Forestry Commission to be planted. Over the space of a hundred years, the agricultural makeup of the British uplands had changed forever. The traditional patchwork of stubbles, heather and grazing land had vanished. Look at satellite imagery of the Dumfries and Galloway hills today and you will see vast blocks of pine trees. Twenty five per cent of the county is now covered in commercial forestry. Here and there, a beige island of sour bog stands out to buck the trend, but it is a long stretch from a series of photographs taken from an Avro Anson shortly after the Second World War which shows stone walls running like fish scales across the uplands; tiny farms and homesteads with different textures and colours in every field.

The microcosmic makeup of upland farms has now blown up. Before, a single upland farm would have had arable land, grazing fields and moorland. Now these constituents are divided by miles. Rather than individual farmers having a hand in arable and livestock farming, entire counties have specialised in their respective areas. It is rare to see a sheep in Norfolk, just as it is unusual to see a large field of cereal crops in Galloway.

The coincidence of a number of changes had meant that in a few short years, the moorland margins where black grouse lived had almost completely

vanished. In the late nineteenth century, Stuart-Wortley was praising that unusual middle ground between open moorland and managed agricultural land. *'It is the Bohemia of shooting'*, he wrote. *'The tract where we have all spent some of the pleasantest of our days in circumventing its distinctive denizens, or in making a mixed bag without the aid of the organisation of a regular shooting party. Here sits the capercailzie and lurks the roe; here abides the blackcock and crouches the hare; here stalks the pheasant and sleeps the woodcock; while from above and below the grouse and partridge meet on the heathery slopes and rushy bottoms of this debateable land, the fringe of the moor'*. More than 120 years later, this 'moorland fringe' certainly does sound like a shooting paradise, if only because it holds a cast list of sporting names many of which have now diminished into semi obscurity.

It is hard not to be nostalgic about 'the good old days'. The traditional layout of farms and commons supported not only a burgeoning rural economy, but a fantastic wealth of wildlife. The transition from woodland to farmland had been most profitable for black grouse, but even then, the populations had not been stable. Peaks and troughs in black grouse numbers have been recorded for decades, but none seem to come close to the final collapse currently occurring not only in Scotland, but also in northern England and Wales.

Victorian attitudes towards the first trickles of black grouse decline were that the birds naturally moved around wide ranges. They noticed that natural habitats will seldom hold a healthy stock of birds indefinitely and that the best way to anchor them to the land was the ongoing practice of cereal farming. In a natural environment, black grouse particularly like transitional vegetation; the plant growth as moorland moves into woodland or vice versa. Mature ecosystems of any kind are, generally speaking, unattractive habitats for black grouse, so while the birds may favour a moor for ten or fifteen years, they are inclined to leave if change is not forthcoming. To Victorian and Edwardian naturalists, any substantial change in black grouse numbers was explained by natural movements to and from appropriate habitats, representing not decline, but migration.

The fact that black grouse move between habitats not only as the seasons change, but also as the years go by had a major part to play in their downfall, not only because shooting estates were less prepared to look after birds that they shared with their neighbours, but also because when the collapse in black grouse populations really accelerated, many people saw it as part of a natural cycle and saw no need to prevent it.

Writing in 1912, the Dumfriesshire naturalist Hugh Gladstone mentioned that black grouse were common, although 'formerly far more abundant than nowadays'. He describes a slow decline which began at the end of the eighteenth century and built speed across the south of Scotland. Without actual figures, it is hard to get an accurate impression of black grouse populations during the intervening two centuries, but the overall impression seems to have been one of sporadic but generally accelerating population collapse.

David Stephen wrote in the *Scottish Field* in 1956 that '*blackgame have been decreasing, generally, for a very long time. In the mid twenties, there were notable, but apparently temporary, increases*', but these were just blips in a general decline. In the late 1930s, Lord Scott admitted that '*we do not know why black grouse are dying out in places once famous for them*', and *The Field* magazine ran a survey of land owners across the country to get to the bottom of the issue. Some commentators worried that shooting was to blame, and suggested a brief trial period of legal protection for black grouse to see if it would help. With hindsight, we can see that many factors played a part in the black grouse's decline, but at a time when they could have been easily saved, no one looked into it in any great depth. Now the populations are so small and so scattered that in many counties it would be totally impossible to restore the birds to any position of prominence.

It is clear to the modern conservationist that the reasons behind this sudden rush into oblivion are solely attributable to man. Black grouse have seen the best and worst of human behaviour over the past one hundred and fifty years of sporting shooting, agricultural change and forest management. Two themes have always been at the forefront of man's management of black grouse: active manipulation and passive neglect. We forced them to rely on us, then turned our backs on them. We reaped from a crop which had been sown accidentally, then when it failed, we shrugged.

Even during the years before the First World War, economists and agricultural scientists were working towards a new future for Britain's uplands. A century of change was quickly closing the door on the viability of black grouse habitats up and down the country, and it was slammed shut by the birth of expansive commercial forestry. Patriotic commentators like Professor G.F. Scott Elliot were looking for ways of maximising Britain's productive output, and in a speech delivered in 1912, he described the nation's greatest potential area for expansion. Explaining his position to the Dumfriesshire and Galloway Antiquarian and Natural History Society, he said that '*Many of us have wandered over the moors of our uplands, and can bear me out in saying that it is only when one ascends to the haunts of the* [curlew], *grouse and blackcock, that one realises how great is the amount of undeveloped land in* [the nation]'. He was right. Moorland fringe may well have been a 'sporting bohemia', but profitable land it was not. Development was coming, and although it didn't mean to, it began to seek out and destroy the nation's prime black grouse habitats.

Since the mid-1960s, the land around my family's property started to be planted up with trees. In line with the rest of the Scottish countryside, and somewhat later than most other areas, huge swathes of moderate quality land in Dumfries and Galloway were bought or let to be managed to the advantage of commercial woodland. Today, three sides of the roughly square area of the Chane have been planted with enormous blocks of Norway spruce, sitka spruce and lodgepole pine. Deep in amongst the mature plantation to the south, trees crowd over a shattered line of grouse butts where the unbroken county record of 367 red grouse were shot in a day during the 1930s. Nothing remains of the original heather, and now the arching trees creak and sway overhead on this forgotten corner of local sporting history. Again, it is hard not to feel a twinge of nostalgia for the loss, but land is there to be used and ghostly memories cannot be allowed to obstruct the fact that profits are a major guiding force for landowners everywhere in the world.

Thick walls of impenetrable trees run for miles along our boundary fences, making the Chane into the tip of a peninsula of moor in a sea of trees; a boggy pit amidst the treetops. The Forestry Commission is a major employer in Dumfries and Galloway, and commercial arboriculture has changed the county forever. Remembering that black grouse were originally semi-woodland birds, this transformation in land use should have been a tremendous boost, but the truth has been rather different. There is no doubt that the falling away of traditional farming practices and the dissolution of gamekeeping in the uplands had a major hand to play in the gradual decay of black grouse numbers

until the 1960s, but, unknowingly, the bid to put the moorland fringe to work has provided the *coup de grace*.

As Scott Elliot had foreseen in 1912, much of what was planted during the second half of the twentieth century was marginal moorland, white hill and peat bog, all ideal habitats for black grouse. After draining, the land was ploughed and planted with young pines, releasing the nutrients trapped in the soil and bringing about an explosion of prosperity amongst heather and blaeberry. At the same time, forest roads made from locally quarried hard core exposed miles of easily-accessible grit which the birds flocked to. The short saplings provided shelter and camouflage for black grouse broods, while an abundance of nutritious undergrowth gave rise to a sudden increase in the failing population.

By the early 1950s, individual sportsmen were beginning to wonder if, in the light of continued decline, black grouse should continue to be shot. Just twenty years later, they had staged an astonishing return thanks to hundreds of thousands of acres of new plantations across their traditional haunts. In the space of sixty years, Scotland's tree coverage leapt from just 3% to 12%. It was as if black grouse had been thrown a lifeline, and the very regeneration of soil and plant life made the future look sunny for the ailing population.

However, it was not to last. Black grouse had earned a reputation as pests to forestry as early as the mid-nineteenth century, when the Duke of Argyll allowed visiting sportsmen to shoot as many birds as they liked to conserve his young plantations. Statistics published in the late 1960s showed that, during bad winters in some areas, up to 80% of young trees can be destroyed by black grouse landing on their leader shoots, spoiling the shape of the tree and ruining the forest's ability to produce quality mature timber.

Despite the fact that they spend much of the winter feeding on buds on some of the most precariously positioned twigs and branches, black grouse are appallingly clumsy in trees. They fall and stumble through the obstacles presented by tender willow branches and the catkinned tops of birches. Often, the first indication you will get of a blackcock feeding in a tree is when it appears to fall out of it, saving itself at the last moment with a noisy clatter of black and white striped wings. The birds were destroying young commercial pine trees by blundering into them, landing on the tender leaders and snapping them off, then wandering around through the youngest trees, pecking off buds and making a nuisance of themselves.

When I began to learn about black grouse, discovering that they had once been seen as pests seemed like an outrageous idea. How those bold birds at the lek could ever be less than admirable was a total mystery. I was righteously delighted to find that the traditional idea of black grouse attacking and putting off red grouse was largely a fallacy, but could not get over the certainty that they had once operated as agricultural pests. As time went by and I got to know the birds, I started to get a better idea of them as a species. Relying solely on unqualified personal observation to diagnose it, blackcock appear to have a seasonal form of schizophrenia, making them alternate between periods of stunning bravado and skulking mischief.

In their 'bravado', they are the stuff of magazine covers; picture perfect and proud. My first impressions of black grouse were taken from the lekking fields, where swollen wattles were the order of the day. You could imagine that, if you were to suggest to a lekking blackcock that it had ever done anything wrong, it would turn up its beak and sniff as if appalled by the very suggestion. The truth is that this anthropomorphised 'personality' is actually a very transient one. They look their best for a few months of the year, but throughout the autumn and into the winter, they are hardly even the same birds. It would be easy to describe them as Jekyll and Hyde, but the implication of that comparison is to apply human values of good against evil. With black grouse, it is simply a matter of sexual hormones.

The resplendent, metallic blue blackcock in April seems like a different species to his cowering, brown headed fool of a counterpart in July, but the nobility of the former is a short lived and sexually necessary characteristic. Nowhere in natural history books will you see photographs of blackcock as slender-necked, wily creatures, but that is how they appear for the majority of the year. As July comes in, the feathers in a blackcock's head fall out and he is left partially bald. As part of his moult, he adorns himself with a scruffy red-brown helmet and passes his days lurking in the deepest reaches of a bog, where valerian and meadowsweet crowd over him until he is nothing more than a romantic memory of spring. In the same way, a greyhen will lose her delicate markings in the height of summer and, when lying still, resembles a coir doormat which has been fed through a lawnmower. By winter, the blackcock is cunning and careful, avoiding human contact at all costs and slipping invisibly between stands of dead bracken and rush.

Black grouse are capable of wreaking tremendous damage on agricultural and commercial activities, but the shining, glossy figure of spring is not responsible. It is his dull, timorous alter-ego. From my perspective, both halves of a black grouse's personality are equally fascinating, but for a forester as for a cereal farmer, the greed and clumsy thoughtlessness of the birds throughout the majority of the year simply cannot be ignored.

Forest managers found it difficult to formulate a unilateral policy on black grouse as pests, because the birds have an unpredictable attitude towards commercial pine trees. Regional variations meant that some birds would eat certain tree species more than others, and it became very hard to calculate precisely what damage was being done. Out of 337 plantations surveyed for black grouse damage in 1968, only twenty percent reported an impact which they described as 'serious'. It was clear that black grouse could pose a threat to commercial forestry, but the danger was unpredictable and transient. Many foresters in badly affected areas organised drives in which black grouse could be shot very hard during the winter to keep the numbers down, and the birds earned themselves few friends during the intensified periods of planting in the 1960s.

Presenting official policy in a leaflet entitled Blackgame, the Forestry Commission explained that *'there are many districts in which black game are barely holding their own, and in such places, the disadvantages of minor damage to timber crops should be weighed carefully against the loss of a fascinating native bird that has some value for sport'*. The Commission recommended that planters should use their common sense to protect their trees from black grouse, taking care to position nurseries away from remote and isolated positions. They carried out experiments with dipping vulnerable buds in lime solutions to make them taste unpleasant, and they even grew pine trees in vast cages to seal the black grouse out altogether, but it was quickly and predictably noted that the costs involved in both of these practices were prohibitive.

The management of the Forestry Commission may have had some sympathy for black grouse, but the men on the ground and several private foresters appear to have had far less patience. While researching this book, I have spoken to a number of former foresters who shot black grouse on the ground with .22 rifles whenever they saw them throughout the 1960s and 1970s, and it was widely alleged in the sporting press that others were illegally destroying birds and their eggs wherever they could. This informal persecution set up a constant pressure of erosion which many resurging populations of black grouse started to find hard to resist.

The word 'forest' was traditionally used to describe a wide and colourful variety of natural and manmade woodlands. Over the past fifty years, it has lost its meaning to the extent that it is now little more than the collective noun for 'trees'. What the industrial planting techniques created went beyond being unnatural, building an environment unlike any Britain had ever seen before. In time, many of these vast tree farms became almost entirely barren

and incapable of supporting any wildlife at all. Crossbills may buzz amid the treetops and goldcrests haunt the fringes, but a block of commercial pines has an extremely small surface area to provide food, particularly in comparison to natural woodland which consists of multiple tiers, layers and dimensions.

As the trees grow, they spread their branches into one another. The twigs form a tight mesh and close out the sunlight. A block of tightly planted pines is only really capable of supporting black grouse for its first ten years of existence. After that, the birds have to follow the sunlight to the margins. The forest floor becomes a shredded and sterile mat of pine needles, incapable of supporting any undergrowth at all. The foresters initially paid little attention to aesthetics, and geometrically perfect blocks had been allowed to fall directly over the land's natural contours. At their margins, trees stopped suddenly like thick walls. There was no natural undergrowth.

As if it wasn't bad enough, the trees brought even more trouble. The dense pines became safe houses for the resurgent vermin to ply their trades. Crows burrowed their nests into the sterile no-man's land presented by the pine plantations, turning the forests into fortresses. Foxes started to live a charmed existence beneath the new trees, popping in and out as they chose and burying their earths under the needly floor. Uncontrolled by forest workers, they spilled into the surrounding countryside, wreaking havoc and presenting serious difficulties for even the most determined farmer.

The trees lay like impassable barriers across the uplands, drowning the light from traditional lekking grounds and fragmenting black grouse populations into unhealthy and isolated pockets. Gaps between forest blocks allowed heather and blaeberry to thrive, but the straight, open rides made ideal hunting corridors for natural predators to ply their trades.

When individual plantations reached maturity, they were clear felled. In some areas, black grouse showed increases in population after the trees had gone, but these were almost always short-lived. Mats of pine needles take years to biodegrade, and in the period following a timber harvest, the sun had no opportunity to work its powers on the dormant heather and blaeberry seeds buried deep beneath the leaf litter. The undergrowth had died and the nutritional value of second generation forestry plantations had dwindled into nothing for black grouse. In many areas, heather and blaeberry which showed signs of having survived were wiped with herbicides to prevent them from competing with the young trees when they were replanted.

As a final insult, forest management policy demanded (and continues to demand) that a scattering of trees should be left after clear felling to provide raptors with somewhere to perch, giving predators a huge advantage over struggling species on the forest floor. Looking back over less than a century of modern commercial forestry, it seems that black grouse never received the same benefits from the trees as they did when the moorland fringes were first planted. It is probable that they never will. Choked into darkness, black grouse had been handed a grim future.

It was some fall from grace. Over the course of 150 years, black grouse had risen from the homely 'pot bird' to become a game bird 'by Royal Appointment', then sunk again to new depths; labelled as vermin and shot as such. Yet again, their close cultural links with farming and domesticity had played against them, although different regional approaches to black grouse gave rise to varying attitudes towards the birds as a sporting bird. High densities of black grouse were occasionally sought after for shooting, but there was a definite point at which enough was enough. Black grouse straddled an unusual boundary between being a sporting bird and being an agricultural pest, and according to land use in regions and counties, sportsmen and pest controllers were often divided in title only by geography. It seems that a black grouse at lek is a defining symbol of British game shooting, while a greyhen sleekly perched on the broken leader of a pine tree is a different kettle of fish altogether.

The 1960s and '70s brought with them a massive increase in sporting shooting. Catering for the ever-expanding interest in country sports, privately-owned forestry plots let their shooting to syndicates; collections of men and women who wanted to enjoy the countryside but who could not afford to pay for big days at exclusive shoots. Plots of trees came up for short term leases and these were snapped up by modest groups who pooled their resources to rear and shoot small numbers of released pheasants. Wild game was included in the leases, so when a blackcock curled out over the guns, he was treated as a pheasant and added to the bag.

Like so many areas of black grouse conservation, their relationship with pheasants is decidedly under-researched. It is very possible that black grouse can contract diseases carried by pheasants and vice versa, and it is certain that secretive wild birds do not enjoy the company of their noisy, hand-reared fellows. Gladstone proposed a theory in 1910 that *'the increase of the pheasant and its consequent extension of range, thereby making two hungry mouths to fill where the food supply has already been diminished to a point below the proper requirements of one, is to my mind... a probable cause* [of the black grouse's decline]'. This certainly does make sense, but on several modern estates in Scotland, red grouse, red legged partridge, grey partridge, pheasants and black grouse are all seen to live side by side in apparent happiness.

Indeed, it seems that some young cock birds actively seek out the company of pheasants, particularly if they have been unable to win a place in a pack. Rather than live alone during their first winter, these immature blackcock can pick up strange habits from reared birds, including the desire to spend time around and feed from plastic hoppers and feed bins – a trick which appears more commonly in blackcock than greyhens and which adult birds seem totally unable to acquire independently in later life.

It has been argued that the shift from black grouse to pheasants followed changing habitats on upland shoots and that one had no real effect on the other. The decline of traditional black grouse habitats left a gap in the sportsman's gamebag, and he filled it with pheasants, meaning that it was a replacement, not an eviction. Either way, once the black grouse had gone, pheasants held the door shut in many areas. By the late 1930s, moor managers were being advised *'that on ground suitable for blackgame, both sexes of wild pheasants should be shot down as hard as possible'*, but by that stage the transition was almost complete.

No matter how well-meaning a syndicate can be, a great deal of work goes into rearing and releasing pheasants and shoot leases can be fairly expensive. As renewal dates for those leases approached, many syndicates realised that the time to see a full return on their investments was now or never. Black grouse were shot very hard, and because keepering black grouse habitat is a long term business, few people had any vested interest in maintaining wild bird numbers if they would never see any benefits themselves. In the same way that their slow cycles and unpredictability had seen them fade away beside red grouse, black grouse began to lose ground against pheasants as well. In addition, black grouse were a minor concern because guns of the day knew about the big

bags of the past. They believed that black grouse were a naturally recurring phenomenon which needed no bolstering or support. Culturally, the very idea that the farmer's 'pot bird' was in danger of vanishing seemed impossible.

A stuffed black grouse is a common sight on the mantle pieces of Galloway. Dozens of intelligent, thoughtful and environmentally sensitive people shot black grouse throughout the 1970s and into the 1980s without ever thinking that their actions were effectively stamping out the final remaining sparks of one of Europe's mightiest populations. In this way, the black grouse's traditional abundance proved to be its final destruction. I spent a fascinating afternoon talking to an old friend about black grouse, knowing that he had shot dozens in an area of forestry near the family farm. He must have assumed that I held his generation solely responsible for the demise of black grouse, so he asked me if I could imagine the disappearance of rabbits. *'Don't be silly',* I said before I could think about it. *'Rabbits will never be extinct'.* He had made his point.

Throughout the 1980s and early 1990s, the remaining few birds were shot by forestry workers and gathered up by rough shooters and foxes. In the 1950s, David Stephen wrote that 'the birds are well distributed across the Scottish mainland, but in pockets. When numbers become low, shooting soon finishes the birds off, but shooting cannot have had much part in the overall decline during the last fifty years' .

It might be easy to think that shooting is the sole cause for the disappearance of black grouse, but this is far from the truth. Victorians and Edwardians certainly shot vast numbers, but judging from single days is misleading. They shot similar numbers years after year, and historical evidence makes it clear that they were shooting the managed surplus of an unnaturally inflated population which depended on traditional land use. Shooters unknowingly chased the black grouse to its grave after successive waves of change in the worlds of agriculture and economics had prepared the ground. Commercial pine forestation, improvements in agricultural technology and the demise of the rural economy had started the ball rolling, but in the eyes of many conservationists, shooters were holding the smoking gun.

As black grouse decline accelerated, human fashions stepped in to deliver a *coup de grace*. As has inevitably been the case for a variety of species across the world, decline brings about an unhelpful degree of interest from humans with a variety of motives. Falling black grouse numbers brought about a scarcity of available eggs for egg collectors, and diminishing numbers of greyhen nests were increasingly raided as supply started to slip below demand. With leks becoming rarer, bird watchers started to apply greater and greater demands on the few displaying birds, and many local populations must have suffered from higher levels of human intrusion during the vital breeding season. It has even been anecdotally suggested that in some areas, growing numbers of bird watchers were becoming an irritant for farmers as they disturbed stock and damaged fencing in their attempts to see a lek. In some areas, black grouse were deliberately shot out to reduce the clamour caused by troublesome tourists, and yet while it is terrible to think of it, these are all normal pressures exerted by clumsy humanity on a species in decline.

The start of the twentieth century had seen black grouse spread not only across Scotland but into Wales and England too. One hundred years later, that range had contracted by 95%. For a bird that naturally depends upon a wide and easy flow of genetic material between local tribes and groups, the modern British countryside appears to have been designed to thwart any natural recovery in black grouse numbers. Towns, forestry blocks and industrial land lies in an impenetrable mesh across the countryside. On a clear day, a blackcock in Lanarkshire can look north to see the Campsie hills and the Trossachs, but his chances of travelling north are non existent. Scotland's population of black grouse is cut in two by the Central Belt; the barrier of urban humanity which runs in an unbroken line from east to west, taking in Edinburgh and Glasgow. Although only a few miles wide at its narrowest, the central belt is effectively impassable to black grouse, providing a good example of how the natural flow of genetic material and bloodlines has been disrupted by human development. You do not have to look far to find other instances of the same process across the nation.

Today, black grouse survive in pockets here and there, and while some populations appear strong, all have a diminishing shelf life if they become isolated and genetically stagnant. Even during the two years spent researching this book, I came across breeding failures amongst greyhens in Galloway which could well be attributable to inbreeding and genetic weakness. As populations sag below a certain point, this process of inbreeding can quickly annihilate the viability of the remaining birds by reducing fertility rates and preventing greyhens from going down on their eggs properly. Despite valiant modern attempts by private landowners and conservation charities to reverse the historical declines, the business of restoring black grouse has never seemed more difficult.

Our farm in the Galloway hills is made up of sixteen hundred acres of rough hillside. Following the decline of traditional farming practices, it has not been used for arable farming for around twenty years, and heather has been slowly eroded from the hillsides by generations of sheep. Crows swarm across the farm by day and foxes trot the tracks after dark. A fall of snow reveals stoat and weasel tracks along the foot of every dyke and fence. Walled in by trees and smothered in sour rushes, all of the numerous factors contributing to bring about habitat decay and the downfall of black grouse are represented on our hillsides.

PART SIX

Predation

Black grouse, birds of prey and the politics of conservation

Given the fact that the history of black grouse decline in Britain might read like a history of our family farm, as far as I was concerned, finding a lekking blackcock of my own was nothing short of a miracle. The more I got to know him over the next few weeks, the more I began to feel as though some kind of divine and ulterior motive had set him before me.

I returned to watch him lek for a few mornings in the hope of spotting a greyhen or another blackcock, but without any luck. Curlews moaned in the mornings, and the first swallows skimmed low over the rushes but other black grouse were not forthcoming. He moved a few hundred yards from the hillside where I had first seen him and began to use the shepherd's lawn as a lekking ground, bubbling furiously just a few feet under her bedroom window. Lek sites are often quite inflexible, and the fact that this single cock was moving around every morning lent weight to the theory that he was not only alone, but also that he was new to the area.

A general opinion in the early twentieth century attributed the decline of black grouse to the ever-growing encroachment of human interests into areas which had traditionally been wild and lonely, but nobody seems to have told this blackcock that. He sought out the only human habitation for more than a mile in every direction, and spent his days prowling through the busy yard and wandering along the hayshed roof. He yammered at the hens and cocked his head cheekily at the old jack russell terrier, blissfully self assured and confident. When he heard a door slamming inside the house, he would stand bolt upright and call as if he resented the noise and was only looking for some peace and quiet.

Having learned that blackcock will display regardless of whether or not any greyhen is watching, I began to have concerns. Could it be that this gaudy and ridiculous bird was only displaying to satisfy some basic hormonal impulse, quite irrespective of whether or not it might lead to mating? I started to suspect that if he was, we were both wasting our time. At the same time, despite the fact that I was enjoying his displays, a single cock bird doth not a population make. I tried to temper my excitement with the thought that unless he could draw in other birds soon, he was doomed.

A further dampener was the probability that even if he did have a greyhen, he may not have been able to cover her properly, since blackcock only become fully sexually mature in their second year. Despite the odds being stacked against him, I couldn't resist crossing my fingers.

After a fortnight, I passed by the farmyard and stopped in to have a chat with the shepherd. As we talked, a multitude of border collies swirled around us, some clinking chains in the gravel, others free to circle the mindless gaggle of hens which scratched on the grass. A gang of jackdaws hacked noisily overhead, settling for a second in the old ash trees, then sagging back into flight like fidgety children. Out from the foot of the garden, the blackcock began to bubble. He was waddling along the top stones of a crumbled dyke with his wingtips trailing in the lichen. As we turned to look, he popped over the far side and sneezed.

Since it was mid-afternoon and he appeared to be utterly unfazed by the activity in the yard, I took the opportunity to get up close to him and take some photographs.

Creeping along behind the wall, I made it to within a few feet of where he displayed. He had chosen a spot where he was almost completely hidden by a mound of young meadowsweet and I could only make out his red wattles and the white tips of his tail. I settled in to listen regardless, absorbing the rich sound while he throbbed and throttled out of sight.

After ten minutes, a shadow flickered on the drystone wall to my right. The trunk of a huge windblown chestnut tree obscured my view, but two delicate little feet popped down from above and padded carefully on the gritty stone. In complete silence, a pretty little greyhen dropped into the short grass and browsed past me like some kind of magical apparition. It is easy to confuse greyhens on the ground with hen pheasants and in the air with red grouse, but seeing this bird at such close quarters left no room for doubt at all.

She had a blunt, wedge-shaped tail and thick black bars across her flanks and back. The feathers from her cheeks crept forward to partially cover and conceal the base of her beak, and although her red eye wattle was completely invisible, there could be no doubting her identity whatsoever. She stepped hesitantly into the thick grass while the blackcock continued to bubble and sneeze behind her, but during the few moments she had been in the open, I had had a fantastic chance to take a quick photograph.

Desperate for someone to share my excitement with, I dashed back to the house to show the shepherd the pictures on my digital camera's display screen. She then amazed me by explaining that the greyhen had been seen in the garden a number of times, arriving long before the blackcock had been spotted. She had assumed that it was a hen pheasant, and had thought no more of it. It was the first week in May, and given the fact that the blackcock was obviously showing a preference for the garden and the lambing field beside it, I started to hope that I might have a breeding pair on my hands.

The natural geography of the farm has led to the formation of a number of bogs and flows, and despite the best efforts of successive generations of farmers, some of these have become actively dangerous to livestock. Cows wander into the quivering mires and then sink to the armpits in treacly black mud. If a sheep wants to live, very little can kill it, but if it chooses to die, then die it will. They sink their hooves into the mud, then wriggle and wriggle until only a few strands of wool remain above ground. What is most galling is the fact that, once they have decided to shuffle off their wooly coil, no man can hope to dissuade them from self destruction.

Around ten years before the blackcock made his sudden appearance on the farm, two of these dangerous wet areas were fenced off altogether. One is high up on the grouse moor and is so wet that it is almost a mystery how the surrounding fence posts remain upright. The other is directly adjacent to the shepherd's garden and comprises around three acres of rough, soaking ground. The past ten years free from grazing have allowed the heather to grow into leggy tufts, and a self-sown assortment of scrubby trees has sprouted in a chaotically haphazard fashion. Marsh cinquefoil, valerian and field scabious run rampant to the height of a knee, while willows, rowans and sitka spruces dot the space. Surrounded on three sides by white grasses, rushes and open pasture, it makes a textbook habitat for black grouse, despite the fact that it is so small and so close to human habitation.

As the weeks went by, the greyhen vanished altogether. I had fingers crossed that she might be laying in the long grass of the bog, and every day that she remained invisible raised my hopes a little higher. At the same time,

I watched the skies anxiously. Wet weather during the first few days of a black grouse chick's life can be disastrous, and entire broods can be wiped out by sustained periods of cold, damp weather. Thankfully, the skies set clear. At night, the stars swept up from the black silhouetted hills to swing overhead as snipe drummed feverishly in the gloom. Every morning, the blackcock's stubborn shape loomed out of the fading darkness, hunched on a dyke or sitting up like a wine bottle in the grasses above the house. He lekked through the buttercups while the dawn mists dispersed and the growing lambs eyed him curiously as he passed. They never got used to his displays, and he appeared to find their bland insubordination quite infuriating. Spring was moving vaguely into summer, and I spent countless hours on the hill, watching and learning.

Greyhens have the reputation of being notoriously bad mothers, a belief not only evinced by the long list of silly nest sites recited by Victorian naturalists, but also by their apparent failure to protect their young. Despite laying between eight and ten eggs, greyhens seldom raise more than half that number to adulthood, and by comparison to red grouse broods, it followed that those poor survival rates reflected badly upon the mother. However, comparing black grouse to red grouse in terms of brood size is perhaps a little unfair.

Black grouse traditionally choose to nest in marginal and obscure locations, meaning that they are far harder to protect from predators than their red cousins. Bogs and marshes are crisscrossed with drainage ditches and mires where little chicks can come to grief in a matter of seconds, while for red grouse on a well-managed moor, protection and relative safety come almost as standard. In addition, the blackcock's caddish refusal to assist in rearing his brood means that the responsibility falls solely on the greyhen, unlike the cooperative teamwork of male and female red grouse.

While researching this book, I heard tell of a leucistic greyhen in the Scottish Borders which many observers mistook for a ptarmigan in winter plumage. Despite the obvious disadvantages which would have accompanied her being white, she was known to have brought up two broods of poults, making human accusations of stupidity and carelessness seem a little unfair. There is nothing inherently wrong with greyhens as mothers, but it wasn't long before my optimistic hopes of breeding black grouse were shattered. A serious problem was lurking in the skies above me.

Red kites were made extinct in Dumfries and Galloway in the late nineteenth century. In 2001, chicks were reared and allowed to take to the air at a number of secret release sites in various isolated spots in the centre of the county. Subsequent breeding successes over the next nine years turned the experiment into a coup for the handful of high profile organisers and funding bodies. Since the project began, the birds established forty recorded nests in the region, and the number of kites continues to grow.

In 2008, I was working with a group of friends and family marking lambs in a crumbly old sheepfold at the back of our farm. It was a cold day in May, and as we manhandled the delicate blackface lambs through the ringing and inoculation process, a large shape loomed over us. A kite was hovering just twenty feet above, buoyed by the winds into a stationary silhouette. It watched us for a few minutes, and we in turn stopped to look back. It was the first red kite that I had ever seen on the farm, and it was certainly the closest I had ever seen anywhere. As it wheeled away over the rushy hill towards the forestry land, I knew that I wanted to see more.

It was immensely gratifying to have a kite hanging over the same sheepfold the following year. Hoping that it might be keen to nest, I watched its progress avidly, sketching it whenever I could and asking local people for constant updates. After a few weeks, they started to laugh when I approached them for information. It emerged that my single kite was actually one of nine. To them, it was no longer anything special. As the spring wore on, I became used to seeing three or four kites at a time, high up over the fields with their wingtips sagging back. It was when I saw seven of them quartering over the black grouse's chosen nesting patch that I began to have real concerns. Although it is obvious that a kite would do no harm to an adult black grouse, I was not quite so sure about the safety of any small chicks that happened to emerge too far into the open. I wrote to the red kite release project explaining my concerns and asked if a kite would take a black grouse chick. I am still waiting for a reply.

To say that the traditional relationship between shooting and birds of prey has not been extremely cordial is something of an understatement. During grouse shooting's period of boom in the late nineteenth and early twentieth century, anything with a hooked beak and talons was described as vermin. Pole traps and bird limes were used to kill buzzards and hawks, while eagles and falcons were shot and poisoned to the extent that several species bordered on extinction. The attitude was that, since gamebirds paid their way, anything that posed a threat to their proliferation was an active assault on the purse of the landowner.

While it is without a doubt correct that these destructive days of land management should have been consigned to the history books, it is undeniable that the actions of Victorian and Edwardian gamekeepers had their roots in solid logic. True to their name, birds of prey, prey. They have evolved to kill and eat other animals, and since their protection under the Wildlife and Countryside Act of 1981, they have returned to prominence across the nation. It is certainly no bad thing to see sparrowhawks and buzzards where once they were a rare thing indeed, but there is an increasingly worrying attitude

amongst several conservation bodies that this increase in raptor numbers is having no impact on the birds that share their habitats.

It will come as no surprise to learn that both red and black grouse are a popular prey for raptors. Generations of falcons were kept to fly against black and red grouse, and by the nineteenth century, naturalists often noted the impact that birds of prey had on moorland wildlife. *'Our experience [of falcons]'*, wrote George Morant in 1875, *'is that five out of six birds they take are grouse or blackgame if they are to be had in the country. They are the most easily caught and the best eating, so it is only natural that they should eat them'.*

There is no doubt that raptors preying on grouse is 'only natural', and it has been actively encouraged in falconry for generations. Some nineteenth century falconers felt uncomfortable about sending their birds up after black grouse, remarking that the *'black grouse try a hawk's courage; young ones are easily killed, but the flight of the old black cock is exceedingly rapid'.* Black grouse were not really the intended quarry of the moorland falconer, but looking on at wild encounters between raptors and black grouse was a rare and memorable event.

Sir Hugh Fraser relates an incident seen by his gamekeeper in 1895 where a wild golden eagle struck and killed a black grouse:

> *'In the forest of Strathconan [near Strathpeffer], where I was for a number of years, I once saw a very fine sight of an eagle pursuing a blackcock. The blackcock got up at the head of a very deep corrie and came over at a very great height. The eagle was about and soon after it. I could see him overtake the bird, and I would say that he struck him in the same way a peregrine does with his claw. I saw something drop, but could not make out what it was at the time; then the eagle doubled in the air and caught the bird before it hit the ground... I was not far off, and could hear a tremendous noise of the wings. When the eagle doubled back and caught the bird in the air I would judge that the bird would be as high up as three hundred feet, and when he doubled back I should think he was not more than fifty.*
>
> *Perhaps the narrowness of the corrie might be the reason for him taking the bird in the way he did – I went to the place and found the head of the black-cock; there were about three inches of skin hanging to the head, a tear like what would be done with the claw. This is the only time that I saw an eagle kill a bird in the air, but it was a grand sight'.*

Many other extraordinary historical accounts exist of black grouse being taken by raptors, none more surprising than the discovery of an entire adult blackcock in a peregrine's nest on the cliffs of Bass Rock, an inaccessible plug of volcanic stone more than a mile off the shore of East Lothian. For a peregrine to have flown such a distance carrying a bird of a similar weight is stunning, and it is worth noting as an aside that black grouse appear to have a particular fear of peregrine falcons. It was recorded in the nineteenth century that whenever a black grouse avoided pursuit from a peregrine, it would become dazed and partially paralysed, even allowing itself to be picked up by human hands. These incidents are included for the sake of their spectacular and unusual natures, but they are certainly relevant to the situation currently unfolding in the British countryside.

Victorian and Edwardian gamekeeping has left what appears to be an indelible stain on the shooting community. Birds of prey were routinely destroyed to protect gamebirds and increase the value of let shooting properties, and that ghost has become a rod for the back of modern country sports. The issue can never rest because a few landowners continue to pressure their keepers into poisoning and shooting eagles and harriers. In these situations, landowners deserve to be heavily punished not only because they are violating the laws of the land, but because their actions are muddying the waters of a genuine issue which will never be dealt with appropriately as long as we find photographs of dead raptors in the newspapers.

The fact that popular conservation charities can back up legal protocol by bringing evidence against 'wildlife criminals' gives them an authoritative air of being 'in the right'. There is no doubt that they are legally 'right' in these cases, but the inferred association is that their policy towards raptors is also ecologically right. This is dangerous. The association of 'right' conservationists against 'wrong' gamekeepers is furthered by the fact that, with legal backing, some conservationists are able to command the heavy threat of police investigation as a powerful tool.

Several commentators and journalists have even received anonymous death threats from obsessive raptor enthusiasts for having spoken against birds of prey. In an environment where simply to voice criticism about birds of prey is to risk interrogation and abuse, the conservationists have created a culture of

fear amongst the majority of law-abiding gamekeepers and sportsmen which closes down dialogues and refuses anything but the single-minded belief that the preservation of raptors is only a good thing. In some cases, it seems that this belief draws strength from nothing more than the fact that destroying raptors was bad, so preserving them must be good, and hang the consequences.

Findings of a five year study on a moor at Langholm during the mid 1990s showed that birds of prey killed 30 per cent of breeding grouse every spring, 37 per cent of chicks each summer, and 30 per cent of surviving chicks each autumn. The impact of raptor predation on red grouse is a well publicised bone of contention between ornithological conservationists and game shooters, but less well researched or publicised is the same relationship between raptors and black grouse.

A study in Wales in 2007 tagged and monitored a population of thirty nine adult black grouse. After a four year study period, only one bird had survived. Fourteen had been killed by foxes, which is comparatively modest when compared with the twenty five that had been killed by birds of prey. When asked to provide figures to explore the significance of these findings in relation to work to conserve black grouse in the Southern Uplands, a Scottish

Raptor Study Group was unwilling to help. According to Adamson:

> *'The Lothian & Borders Raptor Study Group was approached early in the project to try and get a picture of past and present raptor populations within the* [black grouse conservation] *project area, specifically goshawks and peregrines. Unfortunately information was not forthcoming. The local RSG explained that while all their members are genuinely interested in Black Grouse conservation, several questioned why a black grouse conservation group should require information on raptor distribution'.*

Refusal to share the figures is symptomatic of a populist rot which is setting in to British conservation, in which conservation interests which do not directly promote birds of prey are treated with suspicion and secrecy by an ascendant and influential raptor lobby.

Other studies have shown how devastating raptor predation can be to black grouse populations, and one which took place in the North Pennines shows that as many as 44% of a sample group were killed by birds of prey.

Admirers of raptors frequently rebut concerns about the impact of birds of prey by arguing that it is biologically impossible for a predator to eradicate its prey. They correctly argue that, as prey numbers fall, predator numbers follow. Both species are inextricably bound to fluctuating phases of boom and bust, and in theory, this is biologically sound, particularly if you take the example of a goshawk feeding on black grouse. However, theory is not practice. Goshawks are the only raptors found to have even the most faintly catholic predator-prey relationship with black grouse. On the whole, it is unusual for a bird of prey to have a single prey species.

Research has shown that 'raptors which live on grouse moors tend to be 'generalist' predators. Ratcliffe (1993) lists up to fifty different prey species taken by peregrines in British upland locations'. On my family's farm, our peregrines may take more than 25 bird species as adults or chicks. In this way, while raising their young, our peregrines outnumber several individual prey species, including our extremely slight population of lapwings, oystercatchers and golden plovers.

The first few chapters of this book showed how black grouse fell from a healthy nationwide population to existing only in a handful of isolated pockets. Once marginalised into these colonies, they fall into a constant grinding process of erosion at the hands (and talons) of predators. In a good year, they might raise a few more chicks than in a bad year, but the excess will be trimmed off and fed to raptor chicks. Redpath writes that:

> *'generalist predators [like peregrines, buzzards etc.] can have a considerable impact on their prey. If their main prey species declines, for whatever reason, the predators might switch to eating other species. It has also been proposed that generalised predators may prevent populations of their main prey from cycling, as predator numbers are maintained at sufficiently high levels by a variety of prey types to stop the main prey from increasing above a certain threshold'.*

The few remaining pockets of black grouse in Britain are probably not being annihilated by rising numbers of raptors, but in many cases, they are being kept at unsustainably low levels, frozen in weakness until some failing of habitat or climate knocks the bottom out of the population once and for all.

As well as the 'generalist' predator species, black grouse have to contend with increasingly inflated numbers of 'opportunist' predators, such as buzzards. Despite their genial public image, buzzards are not exclusively scavengers. Having disturbed a buzzard from a fresh greyhen kill on the family farm in the first year of my project, I began to pick up information from elsewhere which pointed to the certain fact that, while buzzards are normally idle birds, they have no difficulty in killing black grouse when the opportunity presents itself.

On the whole, they appear to confine their uncommon but dangerous attacks to greyhens and young poults, but I was not surprised to learn that even adult blackcock have fallen foul of low level ambushes, particularly during sustained periods of cold or snow. Some raptor enthusiasts defend buzzards as being little more than worm eating carrion feeders, and while this is largely true, it would be foolish to ignore a store of evidence which suggests that some birds in some areas are a great deal more proactive in their foraging habits than others. Protected by law, it can be a distressing experience to watch the numbers of these birds escalate year after year while black grouse continue to flounder.

As an aside, it is maybe worth remarking that perhaps a key cause for the adder's dramatic decline is the massive increase in buzzard numbers across Britain's uplands. Driving up to the farm one afternoon in mid May, I disturbed what I thought was a buzzard tangled in a length of baling twine. The bird rose from the heather and landed on a dyke nearby, revealing that the string was actually a muscular and mobile snake. It proceeded to stamp on the adder, which must have been little more than two feet long. The shining black scales of the snake were easily visible as the bird trapped the wriggling strip beneath its talons and tried to rip a length from one side of it.

I leaped out of the car and put the buzzard off, spotting with relief that the departing bird had been unable to deliver the coup de grace. The adder melted into the grass behind the dyke, and I wished him a speedy recovery after what must have been a fairly grim experience. At the time, I viewed the behaviour as rare and unusual, but during the subsequent two years spent researching this book, I saw the same buzzard and others in the vicinity catching and killing adders several times, particularly in May, when the bracken stems first appear.

Several major non-shooting conservation charities use evidence carefully chosen from research into raptor predation on red grouse to explain that birds of prey have only a small impact on well-managed grouse moors. Regardless of legality, they correctly argue that it is unacceptable to kill raptors for the financial benefits of a few extra brace of grouse each year.

However, there is more at stake with black grouse than simple shoot economics. We do not just risk a bad season when we allow raptor predation to creep higher and higher; we risk losing an iconic bird species from Britain forever. Figures would suggest that black grouse are actually more vulnerable to raptor predation than their red cousins, and despite their large size, even adult blackcock continue to fall foul of a number of expanding raptor species.

Two independent studies carried out in 1988 and 1996 showed that predator removal experiments allowed black grouse, capercaillie and grey partridges to increase their breeding potential and expand their rate of population growth. The subject is still under-researched, but from these two studies alone, there is enough evidence to make the possibility of a debate on the subject of raptor predation an important step in the future of black grouse conservation. As I write, no such debate even seems possible.

The RSPB's vilification of shooting has driven a wedge between that charity and many landowners, preventing a good relationship between two parties who should be working together. Black grouse surveys carried out by the RSPB are often woefully inaccurate when they come to deal with private land because many farmers are not prepared to provide important assistance to the work of a charity which has its roots in an opposition to country sports. In effect, black grouse only continue to exist in Britain thanks to privately-funded shooting and moorland management, yet the RSPB are on hand to take the credit where populations rise and to cast the first stone where they fall.

In a number of situations where private landowners turned ailing black grouse populations around, encouragement and support from conservation charities has been in short supply. In at least two cases that I came across, wildlife crime officers appeared to redouble their surveillance of the properties, using a resurging black grouse population not as a success story, but as evidence of raptor persecution. Anecdotally, I have spoken to a number of landowners and gamekeepers who deliberately understated or denied altogether the existence of black grouse populations on their property when surveyors came to visit, viewing charity workers as an irritating and unnecessary intrusion on the day-to-day work involved in practical conservation.

It so happens that lekking displays form an attractive spectacle for tourists and bird watchers, and a great deal of publicity in the media has raised awareness amongst the general public about the plight of the black grouse. The RSPB and the Forestry Commission have been quick to support the birds and their work in several areas has been extremely commendable, but their refusal to accept that birds of prey play any role in their ongoing decline leaves large and worrying gaps in their long term plans.

When red kites were released into the hills of Galloway in 2001, the birds took to the skies over the last vestiges of an ailing black grouse population. It is certainly true that, aesthetically, kites fit in well to the Galloway hills, but the potential damage they have already caused to local black grouse populations by stealing chicks and disturbing leks is an unquantifiable setback. From personal experience, I have seen four Galloway leks disturbed by red kites during the two years spent researching this book. On all four occasions, the

blackcock returned within half an hour. Only once did any greyhens return that day. Lek disturbance caused by birds of prey is a logical concern for the black grouse conservationist, but the fact that the organisers of these grand reintroduction schemes fail even to acknowledge it is a worrying sign.

After asking representatives of the RSPB face to face whether or not kites would take black grouse chicks, I was told 'probably not', although several volunteers mentioned that the birds had been seen taking oystercatchers, mallard and magpies, all as chicks. It wouldn't be too great a leap to suggest that black grouse chicks are also vulnerable, but this appears not to have been considered. I was told not to worry.

Surprisingly, I was unsatisfied with their response. When I went on to suggest that carrion is not an inexhaustible resource I was met with expressions of confusion. I explained my concern that even if kites do stick exclusively to eating the existing spread of available carrion, they would quickly begin to take food from the mouths of established raptors and corvids. It would be only natural for buzzards and crows who do not rely exclusively on a diminishing share of carrion to fill their stomachs elsewhere, hitting ground nesting birds even harder by way of compensation. In addition, thanks to ever tightening legislation on the disposal of fallen livestock, kites have been added to the list of carrion feeders at a time when there is less and less available carrion. The inevitable 'knock-on' effect of red kite reintroduction also appeared not to have been considered.

In many ways, the red kite release project, which has now become one of several reintroducing red kites up and down the country, feels like a single minded scheme to promote a highly visible popular bird and generate income at the expense of other, less interesting species. The priority is to install kites at all costs, and the organisers of the project in Galloway have become so set upon that goal that they are blind to all other concerns. In addition, similar reintroductions appear to be taking place 'accidentally' for goshawks in Galloway, despite that bird's studied and documented habit of eating red squirrels, barn owls and black grouse.

There is a tremendous amount of politics at play in British conservation, although some of it is decidedly more trivial and small-minded than others. Several conservation charities have become politically and culturally enormous, attracting millions of pounds in private subscriptions, donations and legacies each year. They are the most important voices in modern conservation, but they are answerable to the general British public, who perhaps understandably, demand plenty of what interests them and little of what does not. From a personal perspective, I have always found birds of prey rather sinister and cold, but I appear to be alone in that view.

It is a certain fact that there is a raw and primal satisfaction in watching a peregrine falcon stoop on a rock pigeon, or in seeing a finch twisting and turning in the short race for survival against a sparrowhawk. Man has a fundamental rapport with birds of prey, and several major conservation charities cater directly for it, which in itself is not a problem. The problem arises when birds of prey are exaggerated to become 'cool' and 'sexy', because by inevitable comparison, their prey becomes dull and forgettable - merely a prop in the raptor's display of aerial 'awesomeness'. There is a particular problem when 'cool' but increasingly common raptors become a limiting factor in the populations of struggling species who have the misfortune of being comparatively dull and unattractive. We sometimes forget that when a peregrine falcon performs a spectacular stoop and kills a bird, something dies.

This is the greatest example of 'popular conservation' so evident in the policies of large scale nationwide charities. The biodiversity of the nation is at risk when some species are favoured over others for the simple reasons of aesthetics and popular fashion, but major conservation charities simply cannot afford to back projects which benefit unpopular birds. Instead, they stack a rising diversity of popular raptors on top of a food chain which contains some dangerously vulnerable prey species.

There would be little objection to reintroducing raptors if they were being placed at the top of a functional food chain, but with many species of wader and songbird at an all-time low ebb, it is potentially a recipe for disaster. Heaping predators on a diminishing number of prey species for the satisfaction of the public may be lucrative, but it is not conservation. The British countryside is in a state of environmental collapse, and more iconic farm birds are placed on the 'red list' of extreme conservation concern every year. The last thing these struggling species need is a human population determined to turn the countryside into a safari park for aesthetically pleasing predators. Some conservationists now release and preserve raptors as a kind of living ornament for the countryside, thinking nothing of what it costs the local ecosystem to keep them there.

It is possible to reconstruct a natural food chain which would sustainably support a wide variety of bird species, including raptors and game birds, but it is only possible to do so from the bottom up. The foundations must be in place before predators can be allowed a free rein, and it increasingly seems that, in their impatience, many conservationists are pushing for the expansion of raptor species before the countryside is fully able to support them.

Though I, as the author of a book on black grouse, might seem a hypocrite for saying it, destructive conservation often has its roots in a conscious human decision to exalt one species over others, rejecting the idea of a natural balance. Birds of prey, like black grouse, cannot exist independently from their complex position in the natural world, and attempts to boost their status will always come at the expense of other species. Happily for me, the very nature of black grouse means that my management work has resulted in improvements for a number of other species. Sensible management of an ecosystem will result in increased raptor numbers in the same way as it will result in an increase of black grouse, but if these increases are to be sustainable, they cannot take place in isolation, or at the expense of anything else.

Watching conservationists arguing between themselves is a sad spectacle. As they fight, their objectives disintegrate and vital time and money is inevitably wasted. The RSPB, the Forestry Commission and Scottish Natural Heritage all do excellent work in Dumfries and Galloway, but the longer the conflict between game shooting and raptor conservation continues, the longer marginal birds like black grouse will continue to suffer. There are clearly logical concerns on both sides of the argument, but unless we can start to look at this problem objectively, we will all have to fight far harder to conserve upland bird species.

PART SEVEN

Conservation

The theory behind the work to conserve black grouse

Having what appeared to be a breeding pair of black grouse living within a few hundred yards of the farm buildings was a definite advantage. The tarmac road peters out altogether as it reaches the steading, and access to the remainder of the farm is limited when your only means of transport is a car that is almost as old as you are. With tremendous good fortune, the blackcock continued his lekking displays within a few yards of the tarmac throughout May and into June, and provided that I stayed in the car, he had no qualms about giving me front row seats. Grouse appear to have a bizarre mental block when it comes to cars, and even the ptarmigan who wander around above the carpark at the Aviemore ski centre look at camper-vans as if they were as much a part of the wilderness as lichen. If I had been forced to approach my blackcock on foot, he would no doubt have flown away at the first opportunity. As it was, I spent hours observing him from less than fifty yards away.

One afternoon, I watched him fly up over the road to land above a sheep-fold thirty yards away from where I was parked. As soon as he landed, he dashed for the nearest reed bed and spent ten minutes peeking out of it timorously as if the world was a truly terrifying place. When he began to dart around between the tussocks, it seemed as though the slightest sound would send him into a fit of panic.

I watched him as he disappeared behind a low rise to re-emerge as a changed bird. His slim neck had become bloated and misshapen; his tail had fanned into a bold puff of feathers and he began to bubble. It was a breezy day, but there was no mistaking that purposeful noise as it was wafted off the wet hillside. Something was bothering him in a patch of reeds above the gate burn, and he worked his way towards it with his chin almost rubbing on the grass.

It soon emerged that two cock pheasants were having a sparring competition in the thicker cover, and I watched them flicking back and forth with happy pomposity as the blackcock closed in on them. He moved like a torpedo, buzzing his fluffy legs over the grass and thrusting himself into the thick of the action. The pheasants were appalled. They stretched their necks as if they didn't believe that he was serious, but soon found otherwise as he pecked and slashed at them, muting his bubbles into a shrill yaffle and sneezing with a burning fury. After a few low dives, he started to charge at them in an upright position, lifting his feet high and wobbling like a scampering penguin. Within a minute, he had driven them both clean out of the area altogether. They sprinted away up the hillside and left him yammering to himself with a self congratulatory mumble.

The victory must have gone to his head, because a few moments later, he attacked a sleeping lamb and was truly horrified when it stood up to reveal that it was more than twice his height. It was only with a great deal of posturing and cooing that he was able to salvage any dignity at all, and he backed away into the long grass with an expression that seemed to say 'I could have you too, but you're hardly worth it'. I thought at the time that, in the absence of anything better to display against, he was picking fights with pheasants, but I now know that the conflict was perhaps more serious than that.

Wild pheasants are resident across the entire farm, and shooting them in the winter revealed that their crops were filled with local vegetation. Although I had learned that pheasants had not ousted black grouse from their traditional haunts, it was perfectly possible the few wild birds could cause my bird trouble, and although he may not have known it in his hormonal rage, he was probably

doing the right thing by trying to drive them away. Black grouse have been found to carry and suffer from coccidiosis and hexamita, both of which can be fatal. Those parasites are particularly associated with gamebirds which have been artificially reared en masse, and although he was fighting off wild pheasants, living in close proximity to other birds is never a good idea. What I found most amazing of all was the fact that, as a usually secretive and non-confrontational bird, he was more than capable of making his presence felt.

The lekking instinct is a strong and violent one, and despite having watched the transition into full lek posture hundreds of times, I am still totally unable to tell when it is about to happen. One moment, you are looking at a slim and elegant figure; the next, it has changed into a raging ball of hormonal violence. The delicate tail fan appears to take hours of patient arrangement, but in actual fact it can be thrown up in an instant, springing outwards like a firework. The change often takes place over the course of a few seconds, but sometimes a blackcock will just appear to lose his cool on the spur of the moment and burst into a fit of swollen wattles and sneezing. It would seem that little effort is needed to keep the tail at full stretch, and I have even seen blackcock in full lek posture while fast asleep.

As a point of interest, an observer can sometimes bring on the full display by imitating the rasping 'sneeze' call through cupped hands. Provided that you stay well out of sight, a single bird in April can often take great exception to the call, and will flutter around the invisible challenger until he realises that he is being made a fool of. In the same way, anything even slightly resembling another blackcock on the lek site will inspire overtures of fury and violence. I experimented with everything from a stuffed blackcock to cardboard silhouettes, which, when placed on the lek site before dawn, were all treated with a similar degree of hormonal stroppiness.

Dozens of scientific and zoological papers have been written on the subject of lekking behaviour, and it is not for me to add to the groaning stack of literature on the subject. Big leks are now rare in Galloway, and due to the fact that my single blackcock was passing his days in pursuit of uncooperative pheasants, I started to look further afield to see the real thing on a larger scale.

It is no exaggeration to say that a number of blackcock lekking is one of the finest natural spectacles in Europe. Waves of activity wash over the gathered birds. At times they will scuttle and hop to such an extent that the lek site becomes an overwhelming tangle of bodies. At others, they bumble slowly and thoughtfully back and forth like old men who know that they are

angry but can't quite recall why. Interspersed between these alternating phases are motionless periods of sulking, pouting and glaring at one another.

Blackcock will lek throughout the year, although the intensity of the performance varies. Even in the dark days of January, cock birds will devote a few minutes each morning to squabbling and displaying, although their wattles are not fully erect and their hearts clearly are not in it. A period of semi-intensive lekking takes place in the Autumn, and this is probably a result of shortening day lengths and a desire to drive home the pecking order to new recruits. It may also serve to let itinerant greyhens know where the leks will be held in the Spring, although no females will directly visit these Autumn displays.

Outside the lek, black grouse are often largely silent. I have heard a variety of hen like clucks, giggles and chattering from both greyhens and blackcock, but when the time comes to put on a display, sound plays a major part in the performance. The low bubbling note is made by vibrating specially adapted air pouches in the throat, and the 'three part coo' (one long bubbling sound, quickly followed by two faster, which rise in pitch like a gear change) is fairly uniform across the entire country. Rasping sneezes take place between short periods of bubbling, rather like the bell at the end of a typewriter's line. The sneeze takes such an effort to produce that the whole body of the bird is wracked with a violent spasm, which varies in intensity from a small bobbing motion to a full blown beat of the wings. White underwings are frequently flashed in time with a sneeze, and the two must serve as an audio-visual advertisement of arrogance and mischief.

Amidst the bubbling and sneezes, blackcock will sometimes hop a few feet into the air so as to broadcast themselves a little further afield. During these 'flutter jumps', the rasping disyllabic sneeze becomes a formless caterwaul, delivered as if it were inspired by some unforgiveable slight or insult. As soon as the fluttering bird lands, he will bounce on his toes with irritation and look around him as if he is being teased by some invisible phantom who remains always tantalisingly out of sight. This noisy screech brings on similar fury in other cocks, and one fluttering bird can quickly have dozens of others bouncing and yowling all around him.

Serious physical attacks tend to be quite rare during a lek, but feathers are often tugged out, and in the confusion of a particularly intense engagement, bruises and scratches are probably quite common. When a confrontation is on and two birds begin to lay into one another, the bubbling rises to a shrill and unexpectedly feminine giggle as the throat pouches deflate. During actual combat, the chunky neck is replaced by a long and flexible ribbon of skin and bone which connects the head to the body.

The most dominant blackcock take a position at the centre of the lekking ground, and these birds are normally the most likely to breed. All around them, lesser birds shuffle and bicker between themselves, hoping to inch their way inwards towards the hot spots. These cocks must be careful while fighting, because, like a bumps race in rowing, their attention must be divided equally between winning new ground from a superior and defending their own patch from the approaches of a subordinate. The word 'lek' is originally an Old Norse verb meaning 'to play', and there certainly is something close to sporting mayhem when the grave, pompous figures get stuck into one another.

When a greyhen approaches the smart gentlemen in black, they almost burst themselves with calls and coos, and as she moves through the lek site, each cock tilts his straining tail towards her as though she were a magnet. Although they squabble with one another, they tend to treat her with an awed respect, waddling deferentially behind her like obsequious butlers. She wanders between her suitors as she chooses, while they bend themselves manfully to the task of wooing her.

It has recently been shown that greyhens copy one another in their choice of sexual partners, and once a blackcock has been chosen by one female, he is likely to be subject to the attention of others. It is a chivalrous contest, and if the lady has no interest, the failed dancers will merely huff and hunch their heads into their shoulders. Forcing her hand is not an option, and once she has passed, many will peck idly at the ground like spoilt children feigning indifference at a missed opportunity. It is not unusual for a greyhen to require a little encouragement, or for a second cock to disturb the act of mating, substituting himself at the crucial moment by a sudden show of strength, but generally there is a well-established code of conduct and it is seldom broken.

The odd duality of my blackcock's nature became more and more obvious as the summer wore on and he began to ease off his lekking a little. By the time that he was starting to moult feathers from his head and neck in the last week of June, the constant furious bubbling had withered away to energetic bursts of displaying, interspersed with long periods of standing around. With his feathers sleeked down against his skin and bald patches on his throat and neck as the moult began, he wandered between the growing lambs like a paranoid guineafowl, shaking like a leaf as soon as he saw me wind down the car window to watch him. Then he would hear a cock pheasant crowing down the hill and he would launch himself into the air with a spitty scream to land as a different species altogether.

Blackcock will lek throughout the year, pausing only during the main moult in July and August, but it is usual amongst single cocks for their lekking

displays to fade away after the immediate breeding season. It turned out that my bird was a real fighter. He charged down a fully-grown Light Sussex cockerel during the first week in July and later that morning he pecked a tail feather from a curlew who happened to be passing at the wrong moment. Not for him the stylised pushing and shoving of massed leks; he was out to cause chaos and mischief.

All seemed well until July 10th, when he vanished. His moult had been picking up speed, and the last time I saw him, he was scarcely recognisable. Up on the moor, a drainage ditch was being dug in an attempt to dry out an area of disintegrating pasture. Walking through the flowering parachutes of meadowsweet, I spotted a cloud of black dust churning up from the hot soil above me. Looking closely with the binoculars, I saw a flash of black, then a small triangle of white amidst the dust. Without warning, the blackcock emerged from the pit and exploded into a thin cloud of soil. Feathers reorganised, he walked slowly away from his dust bath as if it had done him a world of good. An unbroken ring of missing feathers ran around the base of his neck, and I had to remind myself that this was the same bird who had stolen my heart just ten weeks before. As the tatty brown figure swaggered away into a stand of denser cover, I had no idea whether or not I would ever see him again.

Unlike red grouse and ptarmigan, which moult in stages throughout the year, black grouse sink suddenly into a heavy moult which is triggered by low levels of testosterone. When cuckoo spit starts to appear in the heather in early July, a blackcock will begin to look rather shabby. They grow some feathers on their heads and backs which would usually be characteristic of a greyhen, and they assume a dull 'eclipse' plumage which leaves them very weak on the wing. Although their tails are usually back in place by the end of September, many cocks still carry beige and brown feathers into November, as well as white eye-liner on their lower lids. In the name of self preservation, they hide themselves away in the undergrowth throughout the early days of the process, and my bird's disappearance was not totally unexpected. As the weeks went by and his absence started to become more and more noticeable, I assured myself that it was all to be expected and that he would re-emerge after his moult in August. The pessimist in me was convinced that he had been chopped up and swallowed down by some vulgar fox.

The summer progressed, and I had no opportunity to be idle. I had been presented with an opportunity to conserve a really spectacular and dangerously rare species of game bird, and I was not going to let the chance go by me. At the same time, I was under no illusions. The birds on the farm were scattered in a hopelessly thin layer. As much as I loved the blackcock, he was what Swedish sportsmen traditionally called a *squaltorrar*, a lone wanderer. Although I had found another two greyhens more than a mile over the back of the farm and disturbed what appeared to be a party of three other blackcock nearby, the handful of birds I was seeing were an apparently doomed vestige of a far greater population. It would be next to impossible to restore them to respectable numbers, but the optimist in me couldn't resist having a try. In the back of my mind, I knew that if I could get the habitat right, it was perfectly possible that birds would move in from neighbouring populations to fill the void. Even if I was doomed to failure fiddling away with less than a dozen birds, I could learn a great deal which might help others somewhere else. I set to the task.

While the RSPB and various shooting charities may differ on some finer points of conservation, they widely agree on the general principles of black grouse habitat management, and after looking through several books and information guides, I felt like I had a fair idea of what I could do on the farm to help. However, black grouse habitat is the subject of an enormous and often bewilderingly technical research. My very basic grasp of the facts says little about the tremendous amount of scientific research and labour put in every day by conservationists up and down the country, and I am certainly in no position to produce a technical guide for encouraging populations to resurge. As a sportsman and amateur naturalist, the best I can offer is an outline of the basic principles of black grouse conservation, and it is for the reader to look into the ongoing study of scientific habitat management if they imagine that it would be of interest.

Looking at past history, farming for black grouse seems to provide the birds with a fast-acting but essentially unsustainable benefit, while planting small stands of trees and managing heather takes much longer but becomes easily perpetuated if the conditions are appropriate. When I came to look at managing the family farm for black grouse, I looked around at current projects across the country for inspiration. It quickly became apparent that black grouse continue to survive in a variety of different habitats which fall loosely into two groups; habitats comprising primarily open moorland, and habitats which are based around trees. On the whole, and on black grouse in particular it is next to impossible to make generalisations, but the moorland habitats tend to be found largely on the fringes of upland red grouse moors in Northern England and Eastern Scotland, while habitats with trees can be found in Wales and western and southern Scotland.

A visit to the black grouse strongholds of the North Pennines showed how the birds were thriving on open moorland managed to the advantage of red grouse. The Moorland Association claims that over 90% of all known black grouse leks in England currently take place adjacent to heather moorland which is being actively managed for red grouse, and once I had visited the vast rolling dales to the northwest of Barnard Castle, it was not hard to see why. Teesdale and Weardale hold the strongest populations of black grouse in England because of intensive keepering and efficient land management.

As I drove down to visit the Game and Wildlife Conservancy Trust Headquarters at Forest-in-Teesdale, red grouse strode along the verges and

cackled at the car. Overhead, lapwings and curlews in tremendous abundance whirled across the tidy dykes to settle in areas of preserved bog and meadow. The benefits of good gamekeeping to ground nesting birds can hardly be overstated, and since those relatively small areas of commercially managed moorland probably have more gamekeepers than the whole of Dumfries and Galloway, it is hardly surprising that black grouse too should thrive. Heather in massive swards rolled off to the distant horizons, and crows were nothing more than a vague memory. In Teesdale, black grouse are found on the moorland margins where the streams trickle down from the heights, and more than once I jammed on the brakes to watch a greyhen idly wandering through a flowery belt of moss within sight of the road near Langdon Beck.

Since the development of modern moorland management techniques, black grouse have always been able to earn themselves a relatively easy living on the fringes of red grouse country, but now that heather moorland is an exception rather than a rule in the British uplands, there are potential limits to the viability of these increasingly isolated pockets of birds. The GWCT is well aware of the dangers of population isolation, and recent work has been centred around expanding core ranges to link up English birds with others to the north. The population of black grouse in the North Pennines has its foundations in superbly efficient moorland management which is aimed at red grouse, but since it is crucial to establish interlinking corridors of land managed to a similarly high standard, there is still a tremendous amount of work to be done.

The population in the North Pennines is defined by its association with red grouse shooting, but scientific observers note that it is unusual as a result. Teesdale and Weardale are remarkable for their lack of trees, and the fact that these black grouse survive in what is ostensibly a habitat managed for their red cousins makes them a little unusual. It is only when you get away from well-established modern grouse moors that you begin to see real scope for habitat creation and expansion in Britain's uplands.

The habitat in which black grouse can be found in Wales and many areas of Scotland is a rougher and far less particular form of managed environment. Black grouse can happily survive for the majority of the year without any trees at all, but it seems that, over the years, local populations have taken on idiosyncratic habits, and some birds rely far more heavily on covered areas than others. Up in Glenfeshie, near the ski resorts of the Cairngorms, a healthy black grouse population is supported by a modern form of ancient Caledonian forest consisting of Scots pine plantations and huge silver birch forests undergrown with shattered juniper bushes. The hillsides are crowded with indigenous tree species, while in the summer the valleys become soft, luscious meadows. Compare Glenfeshie with Teesdale and you might be forgiven for thinking that it is impossible for the same species to thrive in both habitats, but the two regions represent opposite ends of the same scale for black grouse. Between the two poles of heather moorland and natural forest is a variety of habitats, ranging from the scrubby cleughs of the Scottish Borders to the grassy plains of Lanarkshire, all catering for the requirements of birds with localised and regionally diverse needs.

In central and southwest Scotland and North Wales, black grouse survive in limited numbers around commercial forestry blocks, and it would appear that the birds have partially adapted themselves to life in the manmade jungles. However, black grouse in commercial forestry only ever seem to be 'making do', and no amount of sympathetic commercial forest management has ever produced a thriving, healthy and expanding population of birds.

At Coed Llandegla in the Vale of Clwyd, a large area of commercial forestry is being managed specifically for black grouse by a partnership of conservation bodies. When the decline of black grouse became truly apparent in the early 1990s, the Forestry Commission was amongst the first to study the reasons behind the birds' sudden contraction of range and numbers, and their 1993 report 'Black Grouse and Forestry' is still one of the best guidelines available to foresters who are sympathetic to black grouse.

At Coed Llandegla, dozens of hectares of spruces and pines have been removed along the boundary of a pristine area of heather moorland, and the felled areas have been allowed to recolonise with birches and rowans. The characteristic 'hard edged' forest has been reshaped to increase the amount of 'moorland fringe' habitat favoured by black grouse, and isolated spots of trees have been felled throughout the forest to allow the birds a choice of different habitats.

It is risky work, because of all habitats chosen by black grouse, commercial forestry demands the most active sense of management. Pine trees provide quality shelter and feeding for a short period, after which time they become a serious problem. When I visited Coed Llandegla in late July 2010, the quantity of food available to black grouse was some of the most abundant I had ever seen. Blaeberry crowded over the paths and pine trees ranging from between six inches and four feet presented a fantastic mixed canopy for heather to thrive, but all that good work will be for nothing if they are not thinned and re-worked over the next decade. There is no doubt that trees are an important asset to some black grouse populations, but managing woodland on rotation to keep undergrowth healthy is one of the most expensive practices out there, and in comparison to quality moorland management on open hillsides, it is far from ideal.

A preference for transitional vegetation makes managing woodland for black grouse particularly difficult in the long term. The birds may well choose to spend time on ground that is becoming a wood, but have no particular interest in the stages before planting or after the point at which trees become too tall. In the absence of a satisfactory way of freezing natural habitat transitions, woodland managed for black grouse needs to be systematically worked in a series of cycles to keep a number of sites in or around the appropriate phase required by the birds. In addition, crows, stoats and foxes can start to present real problems inside dense woodland where it can be next to impossible to winkle them out with the same efficiency as out on the open moors. The theory of commercial forest management for black grouse is costly and has never sustained or improved a population of birds for any length of time, but it is far better than nothing at all. Indeed, with the exception of some Scots pine plantations in the Highlands of Scotland, commercial forestry has been consistently shown to be a poor habitat for black grouse, particularly when those forests are dominated with foreign species of spruce trees.

Some of the financial burden of woodland management is absorbed by the fact that Coed Llandegla is mainly managed as an enormous mountain biking centre, and as I walked through the trees, brakes squealed and cyclists shouted all around me. A constant human presence in the woods may not be ideal for the black grouse, but a healthy revenue from enthusiastic tourists is clearly a boost to the birds and needs to be balanced against the disadvantages. Since around half of the entire Welsh population of black grouse live in or around the forest, a great deal has been done to promote the tourist value of the birds, but they nevertheless continue to struggle as a viable population. Similarly, Glencarron forest in North Lanarkshire is being managed for the dual purposes of conserving black grouse and promoting mountain biking. The two practices do not necessarily make ideal bedfellows, and while conservation projects in well-visited areas create a good public image for the site operators, it is hard to imagine that the advantages outweigh the disadvantages.

The majority of plantations around my family farm are privately run, and it would be very difficult to establish a similar degree of woodland regeneration in the case of my current project, but it is clear that the fact that local black grouse have developed a reputation for spending time in and around commercial forestry is being appreciated. While Galloway currently lacks the large-scale woodland management plans seen in North Wales, smaller scale attempts are being made to build suitable habitat into existing forestry.

From a single point above the big bog at the back of our farm, it is possible to see three separate stands of hardwood trees like silver birch and rowan which have been planted along the fringes of the blocks, and despite the fact that they are clearly far too close together, they are sure to do some good. In addition, while some trees are being felled as I write, an attempt to harvest woodland on a rotational basis is surely making some difference. Drains and grips are being blocked to provide soggy ground for breeding birds, and work is underway.

There is a political undertone to these conservation efforts. At some stage along the line, habitat factsheets have been produced which imply that black grouse actively enjoy living in sitka plantations, and advice for would-be black grouse conservationists often praises commercial forestry. Having been devastated by industrial planting in the twentieth century, there is a certain irony in how black grouse are now being used as a symbol of environmentally sustainable forestry. The reinterpretation of black grouse as a woodland icon not only attempts to justify the ongoing destruction of Britain's uplands, but also smacks of embarrassment for just how badly planned and executed the first generation of commercial woodland really was.

Few forest conservationists acknowledge the fact that black grouse were at their most numerous in the late eighteenth century when the uplands were totally bereft of trees, and instead, the plight of the birds is being swallowed

up with apologetic and in many cases half-hearted attempts to make amends for past mistreatment.

Foresters point to the huge population boom of black grouse brought about by the first generation of commercial forestry to justify the expansion and perpetuation of planting, but in truth, second generation forests consistently underperform in their promise to deliver quality habitat. It is obvious that the trees themselves were not responsible for the boom, but rather the associated benefits of ploughing white hill to reveal vigorous, nutritious undergrowth, exposed grit and thick cover. Planting trees clearly can bring about a dramatic increase in black grouse numbers, but it often does not, and the unreliable nature of the process forms a poor foundation for modern conservation plans. It may be cynical of me to say it, but with a "government" keen to increase the forest cover of Scotland by some astronomical percentage in the next few years, it is quite possible that the black grouse's perceived affection for woodland is being used as an excuse to justify extensive planting, even in areas where existing habitat is already perfectly adequate or requires little more than fine-tuning.

While spokesmen enthuse on the ecological advantages of commercial woodland, they cannot deny that their primary objective is to make money, and woodland managed for black grouse is grossly expensive. Perhaps I have an unusually biased attitude against trees because my family's farm is surrounded by the things, but it does not take an expert to see that a block of mature sitka spruce is good for nothing but foxes and low grade pulp.

However, it is important to remember that woodland is not all bad. While sitka spruce is largely incapable of providing food or shelter to all but the most determined seed eaters, indigenous tree species can be made to produce quality food and cover in abundance. Access to winter feeding on birches and alders not only provides a welcome nutritional boost for black grouse during the short days of winter, but evidence now seems to point to the fact that trees are vital to black grouse survival in other ways. Traditional accounts of black grouse behaviour mention the fact that the birds, like red grouse and ptarmigan, are able to build caves under the snow during the harder days, but during extreme cold, populations of black grouse come under real threat from exposure.

During the frozen winter of 2009/2010, almost half the population of black grouse being monitored by the Game and Wildlife Conservancy Trust in the comparatively treeless North Pennines were killed off by heavy snows and a continuous blanket of frost which lay on the ground for several weeks. Researchers noticed how birds with access to woodland consisting of birches, Scots pines and even sitka spruces fared much better during the same winter, and other study groups like that at RSPB Geltsdale recorded a greater survival rate due to nearby trees. The winter of 2009/2010 was unusually cold, but having shelter and a degree of insulation from the biting winds seems to have made a real difference to black grouse survival.

Also, as an example of regional diversity in behaviour, it seems that black grouse can use trees to their advantage in an unexpected way. Like red grouse and a variety of other moorland birds, black grouse roost on the ground. This makes them extremely vulnerable to foxes and stoats, both of which spend much of their time hunting with noses pressed closely to the undergrowth. It does not take much to surprise a sleeping bird, and while many ground roosting birds will face into the wind so that their feathers will not be ruffled and release any tell-tale scents, accidents frequently happen. Greyhens often encourage their broods to roost with them in trees during their first few weeks, but as a general rule, adult birds will always roost on the floor.

Except in Galloway. An abnormally high concentration of commercial forestry and woodland in the county may well have brought about an explosion of fox numbers, but black grouse appear to have responded to that threat by taking to the trees at night time. On more than one occasion, I have seen adult blackcock and greyhens roosting in a stand of horse chestnut trees while I was lamping for foxes, and while I have seen the same birds roosting on the ground, they are not averse to spending the night in the security of raised cover. There seems to be no pattern to the behaviour, and I have seen it taking place in January, July and September. No birds were ever more than ten or twelve feet up in the trees when I saw them, but it serves to illustrate the fact that black grouse are unpredictable, and that they are more than capable of using trees as an unexpected safety measure when the situation calls for it.

Having realised that the modern agricultural makeup of Dumfries and Galloway is comparatively unsuitable for large scale moorland management like that of the North Pennines, and seeing the ancient pedigree of the Caledonian forests of Glenfeshie, a plan started to form in my mind. It would be nearly impossible to create tremendous sweeping stands of heather on my family's farm in Galloway because of the restrictive presence of forestry commission land and the fact that, despite covering sixteen hundred acres, the property is still very

much on the small side. However, black grouse are still surviving on my family's farm, which shares few natural characteristics with the Pennine dales.

There was no point beating my head against a brick wall to change the land into something new when it was starting to become clear that some smaller scale changes to what was already present could be just as productive. Forestry is a fact in Galloway, and I realised that unless I was prepared to give up altogether on the birds, I needed to work with the hostile and unsuitable environment created by massive sitka spruce plantations. A survey of the glens, dales, cleughs and vales of Great Britain had not only revealed the fact that black grouse often have regional habitat requirements, but also gave me an idea of what I needed to do to kickstart my own conservation project.

What was surprising about my survey of black grouse habitats in Britain was the appalling unpredictability of it all. Textbook black grouse habitat exists in tremendous quantities across the nation, but only a fraction of it is being used by the birds. In the same confusing way, some wholly unsuitable habitats are packed with black grouse. While it is relatively easy to see what black grouse need from their environments, there are other less tangible factors at play. These are unpredictable birds, and the fact that we simply do not know very much about them compounds problems like these.

A good starting point for boosting black grouse populations is to work on creating a mosaic of pasture, moorland and bog. A few stands of trees here and there complete the picture as an insurance policy against a hard winter. However, even if everything goes perfectly and the birds have access to the land, they may not choose to use it. In addition, black grouse on the land will appear to have a constant weather eye out for a move, and will desert pristine habitat for something theoretically unsuitable at a moment's notice.

The entire study of black grouse conservation and habitat management is vast and overwhelmingly complex. After a tremendous amount of research and more than a thousand miles on the road between the various pockets of black grouse in Britain, it is fair to conclude that the birds like a variety of different habitats. Having once had a wide distribution across the entire British mainland is surely proof of the fact that they can be flexible and terrifically adaptable, and I set about my work with the refreshing thought that just a few changes to what I already had could make a major difference to the local birds.

PART EIGHT

Botany

Practical habitat management on a shoestring

Within a few weeks of starting to create black grouse habitat on the farm, I realised that I was faced with a variety of problems. First, while a great deal of the land was choked in black grouse-friendly white grasses, reeds and rushes, a total absence of indigenous trees meant that the birds had very little to eat during the winter months. Plentiful bogs, morasses and flows provided great potential for chicks to feed up on insects in the summer months, and they also supplied soft rush seeds, bog cotton flowers and sphagnum fruits, but black grouse need to be able to feed up in the autumn on rowan and hawthorn berries and pass the short winter days on birch and alder buds. The family farm provided some elements of the black grouse's diet in abundance, but the bottleneck preventing population regeneration was the fact that there was little to eat during the winter.

One of my first projects on the farm involved resurrecting an element of traditional arable farming in the fields above the lek site. As an agricultural novice, I asked around for advice on cereal crops and found that oats were the traditional mainstay of the arable uplands. Remembering great tales of Regency sportsmen hiding in the oat stacks for a chance at shooting a black-cock, I threw myself into the task. Restricted by an extremely tight budget, I coaxed some friends into helping me drain and till almost an acre of soaking hillside. We fenced off the area and sowed a single sack of oats into the sodden peat. As the days went by, the patch gradually drained and the oats emerged. It was an experiment in cereal farming, and despite many mistakes, it became obvious that borrowing a tractor and applying the new learning to a larger scale project was not altogether out of the question. Woodpigeons, pheasants and rabbits later plundered the tiny experimental enclosure, but by that time, I had learned some important lessons about sowing oats on raw peat.

There are two fields near the back of the farm which are gradually eroding into nothing. Each year the rushes creep further and further into the sweet grasses, and a bog is beginning to swell and expand in the far corner of one. The sheep pass happy afternoons in the fields during the summer, slouching around through the flowers and the molehills, but bit by bit they are losing their value. Poised above the big bog, they may well offer stunning views out to the Isle of Man, but both need to be worked. Areas of both have been earmarked for oats over the next few years, but planting the crops and leaving them uncut for the benefit of wild birds is unsustainably expensive. A far better way of filling the black grouse's crop during the winter months is to install a scattering of small birch plantations, which was my next project.

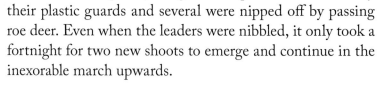

It is well-known that silver birch is an extremely prolific tree, and once installed, it takes very little maintenance to keep it in a constant state of controlled regeneration and expansion. I was amazed by how quickly the eighteen inch long saplings leapt out of the ground, and several had grown even taller than me in their first summer. Their haste was a little ill advised, since many of the tender shoots quickly outgrew the protection offered by their plastic guards and several were nipped off by passing roe deer. Even when the leaders were nibbled, it only took a fortnight for two new shoots to emerge and continue in the inexorable march upwards.

I planted dozens of birches in a small, stony enclosure packed to ankle height with the debris of fallen bracken. Thankfully, the trees were high enough to avoid being smothered by the sudden growth of bracken when it came at the end of June, and it is to be hoped that the two plants

Seasonal Diet of the Black Grouse

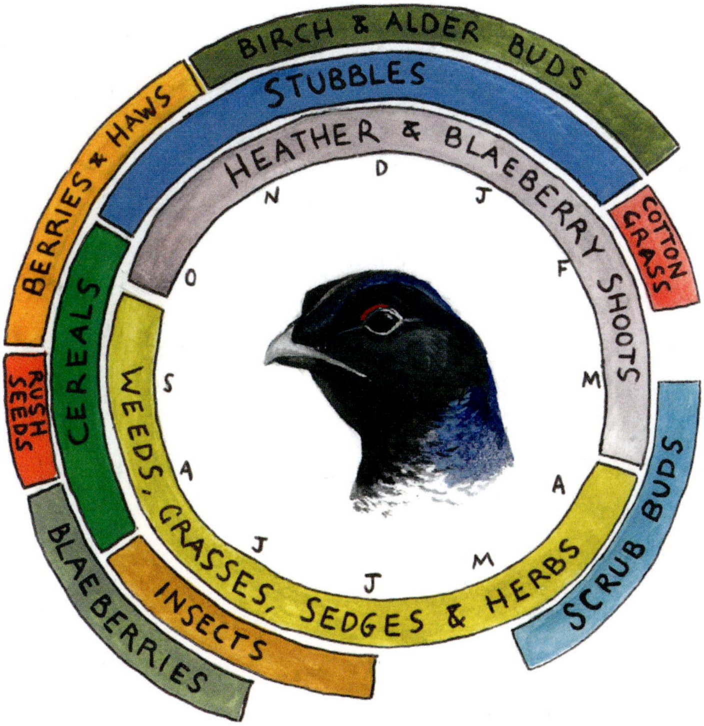

will be able to live together. Bracken can be dangerous for red grouse when it becomes a breeding ground for disease-laden ticks and parasites, but black grouse appear not to be bothered by tick borne diseases. Chicks will weaken and founder if the tick burden rises beyond a certain point, but louping ill appears not to affect the birds. Indeed, moulting cock birds will often seek out high banks of bracken to conceal themselves during the embarrassing days of mottled brown which overtake them in late summer.

I introduced some alders in another area, and wherever I could find a spot safe from the sheep, I jammed a rowan sapling or a hawthorn whip into the ground. Anywhere even slightly boggy was crammed with grey willow cuttings, and with a romantic flourish, I installed a handful of Scots pines to overlook the moor at one of its most picturesque viewpoints. I may not live to see them at their best, but I can imagine how they will look in two hundred years.

It was tempting to plant blocks of indigenous trees, but limited by budget and seeing trees as an option, not a requisite, I made do with a light scattering across the farm. I had discovered that a general rule for black grouse management is not to have too much of anything, and I felt that my random spray of trees conformed to that motto quite nicely. In addition, a few isolated trees across an otherwise bare landscape will attract crows, which land on the topmost branches during their seditious attempts to survey the landscape. Knowing where these swarthy murderers are likely to be should make it easier to trap and dispose of them in the long run.

As well as the broadleaves, I considered planting larches, which provide greyhens with a great source of energy in the spring, but given that the surrounding forestry land had thickets of the deciduous conifer scattered along its outer limits, I saw that box as 'ticked'. After five or six years, the birches and alders should be mature enough to provide winter feeding for the black grouse, and once they have an alternate source of winter food, it will become possible to lay off installing sacrificial crops. The willows should come into their own with tempting green springtime buds, while the rowans and hawthorns look set to provide plentiful autumn berries within the decade.

As well as the birches, I spent some time sourcing and planting juniper. Juniper is quite a common plant to find in garden centres, but most horticultural varieties have been hybridised and meddled with to produce low growing shrubs for rockeries. The true indigenous species has become quite rare in the wild in Britain, and finding the naturally occurring local variety for sale, even from nurseries, is becoming quite a hard task.

Juniper is an extraordinary tree, and seems to be incapable of deciding whether to stand up or fall down. As a compromise, it does a little of both, and neither to any satisfactory extent. Single shoots rise ten or fifteen feet into the air while others from the same tree crawl through the undergrowth, smothered by brambles and honeysuckle. For upland situations, juniper trees not only provide large quantities of berries for birds over the winter, but in their younger years, they grow extremely thickly, giving great cover for birds and wildlife. As an aside, it has been noticed by sporting writers that the flesh of birds found feeding on juniper berries has a very unusual flavour. In a diet combined with pine needles, black grouse and capercaillie which had fed on

Juniper

the berries were often put off the menu altogether by several observers, who disgustedly compared the flavour of the meat to turpentine.

The Chane has a single narrow strip of woodland almost in its centre. Four hundred yards long and around thirty wide, it was planted in the late 1980s to provide shelter for the sheep. In the winter, the persistent winds seem to magnify themselves on the moors, and half an hour without gloves will reduce even the most calloused fingers to a bundle of trembling purple sausages. Sinuses throb and freezing tears dribble down crimson cheeks as, digit by digit, limb by limb, the human body begins to shut down. The sheep burrow themselves in beneath the hanging branches of the wood at night, pressing their bottoms against the rabbit net fence to leave hollow spheres in the snow when the short day arrives and they wander out into the crispy wasteland.

The mixed combination of sitka spruces and lodgepole pines had been fenced off from the stock for twenty years. The trees were around thirty feet high, and great banks of heather and blaeberry reared from the narrow fringes. Inside the plantation, it was a very different story. The lower branches had become a dark meshwork of serrated edges and pointy tips. The shed needles had stacked themselves into a pad of sterile organic material almost six inches deep. Nothing was growing except two or three small patches of moss, and when autumn came, a cornucopia of slimy toadstools crept out of the soil and opened up like foul umbrellas.

Since the wood had been designed only to shelter the sheep, it was never thinned or maintained. Here and there, a young tree had died and the break in the regular lines had left a gap in the evergreen canopy. Crowded into these narrow spaces, whispy strands of declining blaeberry had strained themselves into shoots almost three feet high, searching for the light which was gradually closing above them. At a first glance, the wood looked useless. I had learned that black grouse use plantations as long as the trees allow undergrowth to flourish amongst them, but by the time I came to assess the wood's potential, that point had long since passed. The wood was not only physically impenetrable to black grouse, but it was devoid of any quality feeding materials. It was time to take active steps.

Despite the wood's small size, the few birds on the farm were sure to benefit from any help I could offer, so I took a leaf out of Coed Llandegla's book and set about managing the prickly trees with gusto, breaking up its rectangular shape and allowing the dead earth to regenerate. Dumfries and Galloway has more commercial forestry than any other county in Great Britain, and I planned to use this small block of tightly planted trees to experiment with techniques used to convert bland trees into interesting habitat. After all, if the birds have a future in this county, it has to exist alongside commercial forestry operations. The situation is far from ideal, but it cannot be changed now.

The shape of the wood was on my side. A long narrow strip meant that brashing the lower branches to a height of around six feet allowed a great deal of sunlight to wash right through the enclosed ground. Each branch I cut away revealed more of the distant horizon, and working from inside the wood gave me the pleasant feeling of 'burrowing' through the undergrowth. Wherever it was possible, clumps of trees were taken out altogether, and I stacked the fallen brash into piles so that it would not shade the light starved ground. The results were not long in coming. Within a few weeks, the blaeberry had begun to stage a tremendous recovery. Brown shoots produced single leaves, and a barren patch of gangly plants began to flower.

Some areas were completely clear felled, and wherever the mat of needles had been sufficiently broken, the sunlight drew new life from the soil. Each tree that fell revealed more and more potential. A scattering of rowans and beech trees had been planted around the wood, but the faster growing pines had almost smothered them into non existence. Freeing them from the dark needly tendrils was immensely satisfying, and after a few months' work, the wood began to take on a different aspect altogether. Having a limited budget had forced me to discover at first hand that it is possible to cheaply regenerate existing forestry to make it slightly more amenable to black grouse, and I was thrilled beyond all expectations to hear that the shepherd saw a previously unknown greyhen flying into a freshly cleared area of the wood just weeks after I began the project. As an additional bonus, woodcock stuffed themselves beneath the stacked brash to provide a welcome addition to the annual rough shooting day in January.

At the same time, I had not forgotten the red grouse. I built grit trays from scrap wood and set them up in what I imagined were all the most likely places. Some were used, and others were clearly not. I was kindly given a couple of bucketsful of grouse grit which had been coated with a fatty medication to treat red grouse for parasitic strongyle worms. In extreme cases, red grouse populations collapse when worm infestations get out of control, and given that I was working on wet ground which provided ideal habitat for worms, it seemed important to treat my birds.

On more than one occasion, I spotted blackcock and greyhens taking from the medicated grit trays out on the open moor, and I wondered what effect, if any, the medicine would have on them. It turns out that while black grouse can get infected by strongyle worms on wet ground, the parasites do not cycle and develop into lethal numbers in the same way as they do in red grouse. A black grouse with strongyle worms merely shows a vague loss of condition, although too many can have a negative impact on breeding successes. Deciding that it could only help, I set up several more medicated grit trays across the hill, including one in my favourite blackcock's patch. If nothing else, I suspected that a supply of artificial grit would always be welcome, regardless of whether or not the medicine was helping.

Out on the moor itself, I started to look in real detail at the plant life on offer to black grouse. The small coveys of reds are able to sustain themselves on a mixture of bits and pieces throughout the year, but heather can be an important element of the black grouse's dietary requirements during the winter months. Our heather was not in good condition. Small carpets of closely nibbled undergrowth could be found here and there, but nowhere did a stand stretch to being larger than the size of a tennis court or taller than the sole of my shoe. The hill was dominated by moss and white grasses, and even the little I knew about grouse on starting the project led me to believe that this was not a good thing. Ideally, I could have started to burn strips of old heather to bring about regeneration of the nutritious undergrowth, but the plants had declined beyond that point by the time that I came to look for ways of helping black grouse.

Much is made in the world of moorland management of the impact of grazing on grouse habitats, and in order to see what an effect the sheep and cows were having on the heather, I fenced off a small area during the dark days of February. Many conservationists are concerned about the possible damage to black grouse populations caused by unmarked fencing, and having heard of a bird found dead beneath a stretch of wire locally, I was aware of the risks.

Silver birch

Bilberry

In the majority of cases, bearing birds in mind when positioning new fences can effectively nullify the risk of fatal fence collisions, which mainly take place when a fence is thrown at random across a hillside to suit some illogical human territorial dispute. For a bird flying upwards of sixty miles an hour just a few feet off the ground, dull wires can be almost invisible, and even agile moorland species like red grouse can be hard hit by new fences. A possible solution is to mark fences with metal or plastic tags, but in my case, a smaller scale was needed. I went immediately to the nearest charity shop and bought a revolting silk paisley pattern blouse for seventy five pence. I happily shredded it into long strips which were then tied at intervals between the wires. Letting flying birds know that there is an impassable obstacle between new fenceposts is the most important thing, and, touch wood, the blouse has served its purpose remarkably well over the past eighteen months.

Nature works quickly in the uplands. Within weeks, weird silver cones had emerged from the bog inside the fence. They grew on raised stalks, shooting upwards in a matter of days, while outside the galvanised strands, the moor remained as it had been; barren and inscrutable. Grasses emerged and still the silver cones rose, squirting out yellow sprays of pollen and rising irresistibly. It was only in mid May that I realised what they were. The cones became fragile and fibrous. The silvery sheen fell away and the small heather enclosure filled with a mass of bobbing white shapes. It was bog cotton; hare's tail cotton grass, and it was growing with a focussed concentration inside the enclosure.

Although I didn't appreciate the significance of it at the time, the silver cones had been the flowering part of the plant. Packed with protein, phosphorous and sugars, the stiff little shapes are a highly prized food for black faced sheep, and they emerge as some of the first decent grazing in the dark days of early spring. The hungry sheep fall on the flowers and grind them into nothing, but livestock are not the only ones to benefit from the early feast. Red and black grouse make good use of the bog cotton flowers, and they are an important food source for breeding females who need to build up their energy before the spring. A friend in the Borders observed that

Cotton grass

rather than eating the actual flower, black grouse appear to prefer a short white section of the stalk immediately beneath it, presumably because it is more tender than the fibrous cone.

Knowing that sheep eat heather makes it obvious that they go into direct competition with black grouse during the winter months, but it was only when I saw the plants that the stock had not eaten that I realised what an impact they were having on the moor. Before that moment, I had only seen them as passive grazers, moving idly across the bog with a mouthful of ambiguous cud. I had not realised that they are clever and selective feeders, choosing only the best morsels precisely at the point at which they are most able to provide energy.

As the summer progressed, many species of meadow flower grew on far stronger in the enclosed area than they did elsewhere. Ragged robin and bog asphodel showed particularly prominently, as well as ericaceous shrubs like cowberry, crowberry and wild cranberry. Most importantly, I began to see a real improvement in the heather. One of my first lessons on starting the project was to learn the differences between the various different kinds of heather. Mercifully, I only had to deal with two species present on the farm; cross-leaved heather and ling. Now that I know how to tell the difference between the two, it seems remarkable that I couldn't always do it, but the two plants are ostensibly similar in many ways. Both favour acidic soils and both produce purple flowers in the summer, but the actual structures of the plants are very different. Cross leaved heather prefers wet ground and flowers towards the end of June or at the beginning of July, with large closely bundled groups of cylindrical flowers at the very end of each shoot. By comparison, ling flowers in early August, showing itself as the archetypal symbol of heather moorland with a stack of widely gaping pink flowers along the length of each shoot. Black grouse mainly use ling, and my experimental area had been placed largely over an area of the depressed plant.

Throughout June and into July, the green ling edged further and further up from the peat, while the deer grass rose all around it. Outside the fence, the situation was much the same although the deer grass was being noticeably grazed. The first indication of real progress on the heather was in the first week in August. While the cross-leaved heather had been out in small tufts for a

Snipe 'drumming'

few weeks beforehand, the ling was just starting to show tiny white specks, which on closer inspection appeared to be miniature buds.

The ling continued to rise, but it was overshot by the towering deer grass and soon became partially shaded by it. In amongst the undergrowth inside the enclosure, a warm and vaguely concealed carpet of pink flowers began to emerge. The colour and concentration of these tiny blooms amply rewarded the effort of building the fence, and while it had been partially obscured by deer grass, the plants continued to grow through it without much trouble. Some shoots had risen by as much as five inches in the first summer, and after two seasons, the purple carpet was stunning by comparison to the empty surroundings.

Outside the enclosure, there was little change. Sheep feed on the flowering tips of ling, munching up the important flowers and restricting the plant's ability to reproduce and expand. Starting in late August, they begin to exert real pressure on heather throughout the autumn and winter. Thankfully, my family's farm is not overgrazed, but even the small amount of livestock on the land was having an appreciable effect not only on the heather, but also on valuable grasses and plants. A little attention to where the stock is grazing and the possibility of taking sheep off the hill altogether over the winter could make a real difference to the quality of the undergrowth.

Cross-leaved heather *Ling*

My initial response was to expand the area of experimentation to make a noticeable impact on the moor. I reasoned that if I could stock-proof ten acres, for example, I would start to see large scale improvements. However, it appears not be as simple as that. The property is used to graze cattle during the summer, and while I raged to see my 'cattle proof' tree guards reduced to ruins by teams of lumbering Galloway cows, I have since learned that grazing is crucial to the health of the moor. Cows eat some invasive species of grass which are nutritionally useless to black grouse and which can actively smother and kill heather. In addition, it has recently been shown that areas used by cattle have an increased density of insect life such as sawfly larvae which provides an excellent source of protein for young black grouse chicks.

In the same way, sheep only really cause damage to heather when the grasses begin to die back in the autumn, and their ability to selectively prune certain species of grass and young trees during the summer is an active bonus. Provided that they are not kept in unsuitable numbers, livestock farming can and should go hand in hand with black grouse habitat management. Britain's uplands would certainly be a poorer place without any livestock whatsoever, and historically, black grouse, black faced sheep and black Galloway cattle go hand in hand as important (and coincidentally monochromatic) cultural symbols of southern Scotland.

By the end of August, the patchy heather was showing scattered flowers on our hillsides and an improvised day at snipe had been dutifully carried out to commemorate the glorious twelfth. The blackcock had still not reappeared, and I was more certain than ever that he had gone to meet his maker. In some ways, I was glad. I had grown so attached to him that I found myself worrying about him, and the thought that he had gone to the great lekking ground in the sky took some of the constant concern away. It was on the twentieth of August, the first day of black grouse shooting season, that I noticed a dull shape in the distant rushes above the farm. He was back, but with a rough brown head and no tail, it was not quite the joyous reunion I had hoped for. I watched the uncomfortable figure for a few minutes as it pecked idly at a buttercup before swaying awkwardly off into a tall stand of purple moor grass.

All the work I had done on researching black grouse habitat had been fascinating, but since my favourite blackcock had vanished, I found that I was losing steam a little. Nothing was more rewarding than, after a five mile walk around the hill to keep the roe deer back from my trees on a cold, damp morning, to look up and see the blackcock or one of the greyhens watching my progress from some distant vantage point. As soon as they had vanished, they became an abstract concept, and while I did not mind labouring for the greater good of a future black grouse population, my patience is notoriously short. I am not yet old enough to do things which will not show fruit within a short period of time, and I increasingly found that I was getting distracted by other projects. A few days after the blackcock reappeared, I saw the greyhen accompanied by a single shadowy figure in the long grass behind the old hayfield.

It was game on again.

PART NINE

Vermin

The theory of vermin control

Vermin control demands hour after hour of patient and laborious work, but its importance cannot be underestimated. Black grouse once existed in every county in Great Britain. They have shown that they can be prolific in a variety of fascinating and complex environments, but they stand no chance unless local populations of stoats, weasels, foxes and carrion crows are carefully monitored and systematically dealt with. Work to plant trees, manage heather and sow sacrificial crops is effectively wasted without vermin control.

The gamekeeper's job, reduced to its simplest terms, involves providing birds with food and preventing them from becoming food. Nothing is more damaging to a struggling population of any species than to suffer the constant grinding process of erosion brought about by an exposure to predators, and shifting that weight is vital. Even today, black grouse are present in some areas and not in others, despite the fact that vegetation and topography are essentially identical. Often, the only difference is in whether or not predators are being controlled.

Having a vague understanding of how important the challenge of vermin control can be, I set to the task with uncertainty. Marching around the farm as the seasons revolved into autumn gave days of increasingly engaging and personal entertainment. Looking closely, I saw that the heather was not simply a blanket of woody strands, but that it was alive with fuzzy caterpillars and spiders with elaborate webs. Cock woodpigeons clapped and rode waves overhead as they performed their undulating display flights, and half glimpsed fox tails disappearing over dykes or into thick forestry made my hair stand on end.

One fox in particular grabbed my attention. An old vixen liked to walk the furthest boundary in the last few minutes of daylight, trotting quickly along the top stones of a dyke before dropping down into the gloom of the dark trees. I watched her more than once, six hundred yards away and furiously impotent. Her tracks scuffed the lichen from the dyke tops, and a dark alley into the trees outside the boundary fence was permanently pocked with the mark of neatly placed pads.

Following her trail one late afternoon, I came across a bed of feathers on the moss. They were silver, and marked with horizontal chocolate brown bars. Four inches of greenish grey beak lay amongst them, chewed from a face and left to form a tiny, grisly mask. She had taken a snipe.

Advised by a gamekeeper friend that one of the best ways to take a fox is to catch them out in the first rays of the rising sun after a cold night, I drove up to the farm the following morning. It was bleak and blue, but shafts of purple light lit up the Solway as I pulled to a halt. Although it was a two mile walk to where I had found the ruined snipe, I strode through the shiny dew quite happily as the sun crept higher and my stomach churned an early morning protest. A curlew wept into the breeze from a ditch by my feet, and grouse cocks yammered away to themselves on the higher ground. A handful of skylarks had anticipated the coming day by hanging high up in the sky like tiny Christmas decorations. They glowed golden in the invisible sun while the hollow bog still cowered in gloom.

I had half a mile to go when I saw her. The light was creeping down the trees as the sun rose over the hillside, forcing the shadows down into the wilting strands of blaeberry. She seemed to stretch her neck to meet the yellow rays, and they lit up her white chest like an electric light. Bent double and running behind an old dyke, I came to within three hundred yards and then worked behind a dead bank of bracken until I was directly between her and

the sun. From her perspective, I would have been invisible as I crawled the last seventy yards; a blinding dazzle swamping the hillside all around me. The .243 came easily to hand and she flipped over onto her side with a reassuring thump. It was a moment like no other, and with the rising sun behind me and forty miles of southern Scotland visible in every direction, I curled up under an ancient Scots pine tree and had a smoke.

She was one of many foxes to come off the farm in the first months, but patrolling the land with a rifle on my back had major limitations. Although I was shooting foxes fairly frequently, the overwhelming majority had simply learned to keep their heads down whenever I appeared, and all my work was scarcely skimming the surface of the problem. A few weeks after spotting the greyhen and her shadowy accomplice in the late days of August, I found a mess of speckled feathers in the rushes. The poult was dead, and in one fell swoop, a passing fox had destroyed the product of an entire summer's work for the greyhen. Following a thin trail of pale feathers through the rushes, I came at length to a small clearing where the fox had lain up. A small, fuzzy foot was all that remained beneath the velvety sloes of a blackthorn tree.

To say that I was disappointed is a major understatement. It was my own fault, of course. Having failed to take vermin control as seriously as I should have done, I had allowed that situation to take place. It would be wrong to suggest that foxes survive only on a diet of black grouse, but as opportunists, they will kill almost anything if the circumstances are right. It was an accidental death, but it was one that could have been avoided.

An extremely high annual mortality rate amongst adult black grouse made it seem very unlikely that both of my pair would ever see another spring, and raising even a single youngster into August had been a real triumph for the greyhen. Something had to be done, but taking firm control of a huge area of derelict wilderness was going to be an enormous job, made even harder by the fact that I was operating on an expendable monthly budget that often fell into single figures. A significant part of me said 'why bother?' My research had led me to a friendly estate in the Scottish Borders where I could reliably see fifteen or twenty black grouse at a time, so why didn't I just abandon my birds as a lost cause and head over to the east coast whenever I wanted to see a black grouse?

Although I hadn't noticed it, I had become addicted to the farm. Britain's uplands have a disturbingly irresistible call, and the hill had caught me. I was fixated on black grouse, but felt equally enthralled by any number of

other moorland species. Listening to lapwings calling in the half darkness of midnight in June made my skin prickle. Having to duck as a snipe drummed over my head like a smoking Messerschmitt has become a vivid, electric memory. Everything I did was pervaded by the smell of meadowsweet and the sour smell of damp moss. From the moment I discovered the remains of the poult, I resolved to get really stuck into the local vermin. The only way for me was onwards, no matter what 'onwards' might entail.

The shooting community has a general envy for the lifestyle of a gamekeeper. People imagine that vermin control is something rather like sport, and they make the logical assumption that, while there are some dirty aspects to the job, it is largely a relaxing and peaceful rural pursuit. The first lesson I learned was that it is nothing of the sort. I had failed to keep fox numbers down because I had treated fox control as a leisure activity. I enjoyed my time walking around the farm with the rifle, and while pleasure and gamekeeping are by no means mutually exclusive, shooting foxes was something I did when it suited me. I was dancing around the issues presented by foxes without grasping the situation seriously and pragmatically. Discovering an occupied fox earth in mid-April, I turned down the opportunity to clear it out with terriers because I believed that it would be unsporting to kill defenceless cubs. Instead, I left the earth for a month and then sat out late one evening to shoot them with a rifle. Inevitably, the entire family had vanished into the forest and were never to be seen again.

Having learned the hard way that vermin control is no game, I started to make some headway. If an opportunity presented itself to kill a fox, it was taken then and there without a moment's hesitation. There are many tricks and shortcuts to tackling foxes, but as a novice, it is not my place to even try to describe them. Suffice it to say that as I experimented with various hairbrained new schemes to coax a fox within range of my rifle, I occasionally hit on something that really turned the tables to my advantage.

Open ground is tricky to shoot, since far sighted foxes spot even the slightest suspicious movement long before they come into rifle range. After receiving formal instruction on the subject, I invested in a number of fox snares. Snares have attracted some negative attention in the press in recent years, but without them, I would have made little progress in those early days. It is hard to imagine what fox control would be like without snares, but I daresay that an ascendant animal rights movement will show us in the next few years. What is certain is that the main victims of any future ban on snaring will be black grouse and any number of other ground nesting birds.

One of the first changes I made after discovering the remains of the black grouse poult was to carry my .243 rifle at all times. The simple alteration instantly made a huge difference. I am by no means a good shot, but one by one, crows started to feel the pinch. Mercifully, I had chosen a light little rifle with a short barrel which was easily slung over a shoulder when a particularly long trek was called for. The crows quickly lost their customary smugness as I popped up in all sorts of unexpected places, and I felt that, even if I did miss a few birds, it was good to keep them all on the hop.

At the same time, I began to experiment with a series of Larsen traps, positioning them in likely spots around the farm. The Larsens worked in phases. A week would go by and I would catch nothing, then there would be a three day period during which the catch compartments were filled so frequently that I struggled to keep them empty. Through April and into May, I began to catch up with breeding pairs of crows, and discovering the best places for a Larsen gave me an idea of where I could build a larger 'letterbox' trap.

Carrion crows are the most unforgivable egg thieves, and getting on top them was vitally important from the outset. Nest raiders of any kind cannot be tolerated, and I diversified my zero tolerance policy towards crows to include magpies and jackdaws, both of whom were to be found in healthy numbers on the farm. Ravens are also very common, and thanks to the fact that they are protected by law, they are doing very well. Each year brings more and more of them, which is not all a bad thing.

From an aesthetic perspective, a raven makes a fine contribution to the January landscape as he rolls over onto his back in mid-flight, creaking and purring with a tremendously resonant voice. Often, the call sounds as though it comes from just a few feet above your head, yet when you turn to look, there is nothing more than a distant speck far out in the open. Despite their appeal, ravens can be a real problem for eggs and chicks, and like the astonishingly inflated numbers of buzzards in the country, there is a growing case for the authorities to recognise rising numbers of both species as a threat to wildlife.

As a point of interest, I once saw a raven break off its display flight on a cold January morning to swoop down and mob a solitary blackcock. The blackcock rose out of the rushes like a meteor and streaked away over the hill, leaving the raven paddling slowly behind him, clocking and panting to itself. I can think of no explanation for this unprovoked attack other than the fact that, despite their beauty and magic, ravens are little more than big crows with bad attitudes and anti-social habits.

My research taught me that gulls can be extremely destructive to ground nesting birds, and I began to look suspiciously at the few greater black backed brutes who sat up in the heather during the spring. On Ailsa Craig in 1867, a black grouse egg was found in the nest of a black backed gull more than ten miles from the mainland, and having seen the damage caused to ailing lambs by broad yellow beaks, I now have little sympathy for those maritime marauders.

Despite the benefits brought by the fact that the land is being primarily worked as a sheep farm, a key setback is the torrent of vermin brought about by the lambing season. When the first lambs begin to appear during the early days of April, the visible number of crows and gulls soars. While fallen stock and dead lambs are cleared up with all reasonable haste, it does not take long for those beady eyed predators to home in. Once, I saw a blackback swing into the wind with almost two feet of bloody tissue trailing from his beak. Vulnerable lambs with juicy eyes, struggling ewes and rubbery sheets of afterbirth are all great attractants for winged troublemakers, and once they are on the hill, there is no doubt that they could quickly and easily gobble down not only eggs but the chicks of any number of ground nesting birds.

Some conservationists argue against the need to control crows and flying vermin by recommending instead the creation and maintenance of suitable ground cover for eggs and chicks. Long, leggy heather and thick undergrowth should be enough to protect young black grouse from marauding predators, and in many cases, the right environment is indeed a safehouse for young birds. Black grouse chicks are very nearly invisible, even against scant cover, and since male birds only begin to turn black when they are able to fly and evade most scavenging predators, they can stalk the dense cover in relative safety. It is important not to underestimate the value of good breeding habitats, but it would be foolhardy to rely entirely on quality cover alone to protect eggs and chicks from predation. Thick undergrowth may protect some young birds from above, but without any vermin control, trouble will never be far away.

Weasels are some of the most fascinating and beguiling little carnivores at large in the British countryside, given a terrific hint of mystery by the fact that they are almost entirely invisible. Tiny, well camouflaged and active largely under the cover of darkness, it is hardly surprising that it is a rare sight to come across a weasel, but their wide distribution and local abundance means that they are never far away. Despite their small scale, weasels are sometimes capable of killing rabbits and ground nesting birds, but the real problem they present to the black grouse is as nest raiders, stealing eggs and killing chicks whenever they come across them.

The impact made by weasels pales by comparison to that of their larger cousin, the stoat. Big enough to routinely deal with adult rabbits, stoats are the real gangsters of the moor, thinking nothing of killing a greyhen on the nest and making off with all of her eggs, one by one. Using dykes as passageways across the open ground, they winkle out wheatear nests and grip grouse behind their heads with tiny needle teeth. Stoats sit very high on the list of dangerous vermin species for black grouse, and taking them in hand was my next major challenge. As a devoted ferret keeper, I will admit that I felt a touch of regret when I came to dealing with stoats and weasels. My ferrets must be some of the most spoilt and overindulged animals in the country, and the idea of killing their relatives made me feel a little uneasy, but wasting the opportunity to clear out the fox earth had taught me not to be sentimental.

According to the GWCT, a square kilometre of moorland can yield anything between one and eight trapped stoats in a year. Population densities will obviously vary according to an abundance or scarcity of their habitat requirements, and estimates for an annual catch of weasels were considerably less. Given that I was hoping to control stoats on what would be properly recognised as farmland rather than moorland, I realised quite early on that I had everything a stoat would need to thrive. In fact, it would be difficult to design a better habitat for stoats than could already be found in the crumbled drystone dykes and rabbit nibbled pastures of the hill. Although I had never seen a stoat on the farm, I knew that they were out there. In the same way, hundreds of acres of unkempt blow grass were wriggling with voles and mice, and I expected weasels to feature highly on my list of trapped predators.

Having travelled across Great Britain to see black grouse habitats, I met many gamekeepers from a variety of backgrounds. Traditionally, lowland pheasant keepers are secretive bodies, hiding information behind politely evasive comments. This is only logical, since poachers lurk around the release pens, and careless talk often brings unwanted attention. For grouse keepers, the general attitude appears to be rather more open. Many of the men I met were expansive, informative and genuinely helpful, and one in particular followed up his advice with telephone calls and letters to see how I was getting on. It was to these men that many of my first questions about stoats were asked, and it is thanks to their support that I made a start on trapping.

A few weeks after buying my first Fenn trap, I found that I had caught a stoat as it raced across a deliberately positioned bridge from one side of a mossy burn to the other. A few days later, I caught a weasel in a trap buried deeply in the centre of a little cairn. Bit by bit, I was learning, and I began to experiment by baiting my traps with rabbit blood and small slivers of liver. The numbers rose until I found that I had caught four stoats and seventeen weasels in just over three months. It was clearly just the tip of the iceberg, but having recognised the problem, it was heartening to feel as though I was getting somewhere. Limited by only being able to afford six traps, my early successes prompted further investment, and within a year, I had a more respectable spread in operation across the farm. What I found most remarkable of all was that although I was visiting, checking (and often emptying) my traps every day, I still never saw a live stoat or weasel at any time.

I was particularly impressed with the stoats I caught, many of which were far larger than I had expected them to be. One in particular was a vast creature, nineteen inches from nose to tail and weighing a fraction less than a pound. It was not hard to imagine what trouble he could have caused to a brood of young black grouse, and I checked the rest of my traps with a spring in my step the day that he was brought to book. I took him home to show my ferrets and was rewarded by their stunned astonishment. They fuzzed up their tails like spruce buds and explored their fallen relative with the most graphic interest.

When I asked around about stoats, gamekeepers would often respond by asking whether or not I had any rabbits on the land. I replied that there were a good few, although their cycle had crashed two years before I began the project and most of the big warrens were totally deserted. At the time, it seemed rather irrelevant to ask questions about rabbits, but now that I know that they are the stoat's number one source of food, the question makes a little more sense. In theory, eliminating my rabbit population would put a cap on the number of stoats, and they could be squeezed out bit by bit if a firm hold could be kept on rabbit numbers.

However, like so many other areas of my project, it was not going to be as simple as all that. In a situation in which a high concentration of rabbits is buoying a strong population of stoats, removing rabbits could spell disaster for other prey species like black grouse. It is a tricky riddle, and after canvassing opinion from a variety of different people, my solution was finally reached. The last thing I wanted was an inflated population of stoats suddenly finding

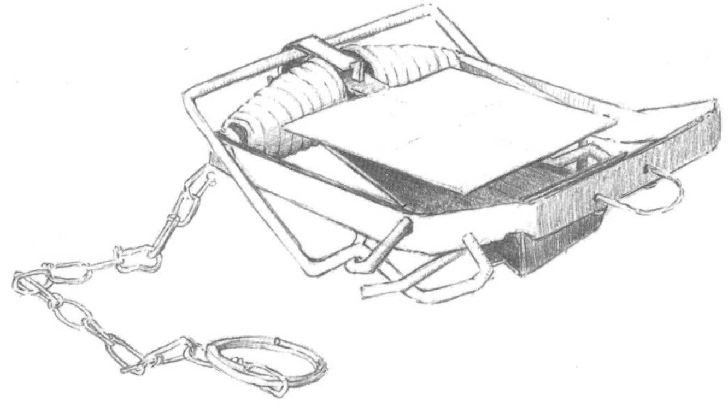

themselves hungry in the absence of rabbits and ranging off into the heather to see what else was on the menu.

To avoid that hair-raising eventuality, I redoubled my trapping efforts and gradually started to take rabbits from their warrens using a combination of ferrets, lamping and snares. In an attempt to defuse the situation, both predator and prey numbers were cut down very slowly, and the process will continue until both reach manageable levels. When rabbit numbers start to return again, as they inevitably will, I shall have to work very hard to keep them at a constant low to avoid losing the advantage of all my work so far. It is still too early to tell how this solution will work, but if I can start to see a decrease in stoat and weasel numbers over the next few years, I will be very pleased indeed.

Learning about the significance of rabbits and stoats, and how that relationship impacts upon game birds was a crucial lesson, not only in terms of vermin control, but also in how everything fits together. It is impossible to do anything to moorland without some knock-on effect elsewhere, and I started to learn that everything needs to be carefully considered and planned well in advance.

My Larsen traps, rabbit snares and tunnel traps were positioned on a two mile circuit around half of the moor, and I started to walk them every morning at first light. Often, I would peer out of the window and see fat grey clouds hanging over the hill from the warmth of my home at the foot of the glen, and on mornings like those, I really wondered what on earth I was doing. Bit by bit, the fun of being up on the hillside was melting away. Deceptive fogs swept in as I walked and washed me up in unexpected places across the moor, miles from the car and soaking to the thighs. My romantic ideas of what it took to be a gamekeeper were being rinsed off me by successive waves of sleet and rain.

It was only on an unusually clear morning in March, almost eighteen months after the project began, that I realised why I was still working on the farm. I had just lifted the top stones from a sprung Fenn trap to reveal a large male stoat in almost full ermine, with only the narrowest pair of brown spectacles to suggest that he had ever been any colour but pure white. The trap had gripped him around the neck and then again just above the hips, and I prised the steel jaws apart and dropped him down into the soggy heather. Looking

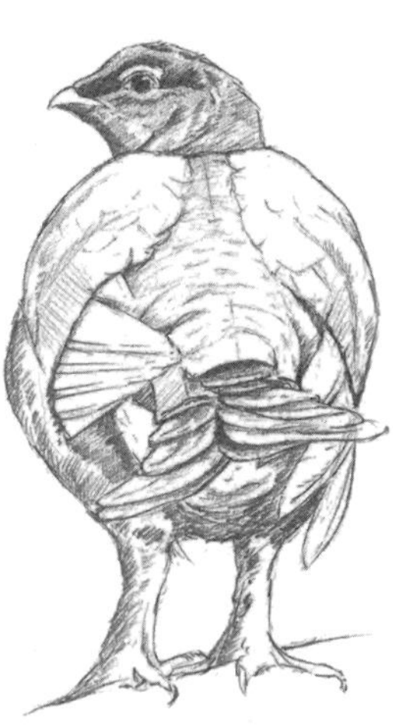

west, the Rhinns of Kells loomed out of the morning like a crumbled dyke. The summit of every hill from Curlywee to the Ring of Garryhorn was picked out with astonishing clarity, while a phenomenon known to hillwalkers as a 'cloud inversion' meant that the broad complexity of the Dee valley was smothered in a layer of water vapour as smooth as a billiard table. Somewhere below those cloudy floorboards, a blackcock was bubbling. The coincidence of sight and sound was magical, but I was not a visitor admiring scenery. In a very small way, I was part of that landscape, and it made me extremely proud.

There is a reasonable school of thought which might argue that if a bird like the black grouse is so vulnerable as to need constant protection from the other animals around it, it is ultimately a doomed species. The artificial and costly removal of foxes and crows from the food chain may seem like time wasted because it fails to solve the problem once and for all, merely postponing the full realisation of what seems to be a fairly logical truth that, in the modern British countryside, black grouse have become intrinsically vulnerable. That idea may be logical, but it is also callous and irresponsible.

To change a landscape and devolve responsibility for survival on the few remaining species is extremely dangerous. Black grouse decline is associated with the general disappearance of a large number of plant and insect species, all of which are interrelated. Black grouse are conspicuous signs of healthy moorland, and in their absence, we quickly lose touch with the condition of less visible species. When a large, highly visible bird begins to vanish, who knows what else we have lost and stand to lose.

The British countryside is no longer wild. Over the past thousand years, humans have destroyed many of the predators who would have controlled what we now recognise as vermin species. Ours is a dysfunctional foodchain, because many of the organisms which regulated it have become extinct. We no longer have large carnivores which would keep a lid on fox populations and few large birds of prey to control smaller vermin species. The countryside has been warped out of all proportions, and only the most adaptable animals have survived. In the absence of so many indigenous species, humans need to be able to monitor and maintain the balance. Without active management, the isolation and solitude of the British countryside which draws thousands of visitors every year becomes truly vacant and barren.

Vermin control should be an unsustainable practice, given that it is costly and tremendously time consuming, but it works because country people care deeply about the most vulnerable animals which would suffer and vanish in our distorted food chain. In the case of an endangered species like the black grouse, it is absolutely above criticism on moral grounds.

In some cases, the balance becomes tipped too far in the direction of game birds, and history has shown us that a moor stuffed to bursting point with black grouse is as ecologically undesirable as a hillside littered with crows, but vermin control is just that. It is not the wanton destruction of every predator species, but control of all to the benefit of all. Foxes and stoats are some of our most beautiful mammals, and no rational human would ever want to see them smashed into extinction. Provided that predators can be kept down to manageable numbers, it is possible to have large, healthy populations of

black grouse living alongside a thin scattering of predatory animals. All the time spent on vermin control every year by gamekeepers across the nation is repaid not only in the financial returns of birds shot and bags taken, but in the continued prosperity of red grouse, grey partridges, snipe and any number of other groundnesting waders, gamebirds and wildfowl.

By the early autumn, my blackcock was almost back to fighting fitness after the lazy days of his summer moult. I flushed him once or twice, amazed by the contradictions of his physical appearance. At around sixteen months old, he had finally acquired his full adult plumage; shimmering blue even in the dullest weather. It was almost uncanny how this bulky and outrageously coloured bird was able to make himself invisible on a hill of rusty reds, beiges and creams. And when he was flushed, he took to the air with the sound of a bookcase falling suddenly forwards onto a carpeted floor, rising like an item of laundry in a gale. For the first few seconds, his attitude was classic; determined, haughty and going like hell. Once at a satisfactory height, his wingbeats became intermittent and lost much of their frantic chaos. Seeing him fly at a distance, I mistook him on one occasion for a cormorant and on another for a horribly deformed woodpigeon. Black grouse certainly have a very distinctive flight pattern, and only after extended periods of watching the birds in the wild am I able to picture that unusually straggling, curious action.

The movement was seared into my memory for several days after an afternoon spent decoying rooks in the old hayfield behind the farmhouse. It was a warm day in mid-October, and one or two cawing silhouettes arrived every now and again to sail noisily along the dykes or rest in the ancient shade of a withered hawthorn tree. Their wings rattled overhead now and again, but I was starting not to notice anymore. I had put my gun to one side and sat, bare footed, curling my toes in the short grass. As the afternoon drew on, I drifted happily in and out of consciousness while the plastic rooks stood obediently in a semi circle nearby.

Every now and again, a small squadron of starlings seared overhead from behind, trilling and squeaking. I started to listen for them, picking up the distant hiss when it was nothing more than a whisper and trying to guess where they would appear above me. After a little while, a different sound swept through the dyke behind me. It was a big group of starlings; it was a bigger group of starlings; it was every starling in Europe, racing down upon me like a flood. I remember thinking for a split second of irrational panic that the hill must have caught alight and that I was listening to wildfire raging through the blow grass. I half stood to look back.

The blackcock passed within ten feet of my head, blinking contemptuously as he cruised over the rough wall and out into the open. His wings wailed like flanker's flags as he beat them twice and seared away into the distance like an Avro Lancaster. I was left with a vision of long, thick wings and a tail that shone as if it had been polished. For a single moment, I had been given an inkling of what it must have been like to face the massed packs of black grouse a hundred years ago. The mildewed, leather bound accounts I had read while researching for this book came to life - if I hadn't already been hooked, I would have been.

PART TEN

Reintroduction

Can an artificial population of grouse be built?

Throughout the history of man's association with nature, repeated attempts have been made to exercise some degree of control over wild animals. Unlike many other wild species, we know of no attempts ever made to domesticate grouse, but as their populations expanded and contracted during the rise of sporting shooting in the mid-19th century, some estates across the country investigated the possibility of breeding and releasing birds. Knowing that they had once existed in force across the entire nation, the sporting press exhorted landowners to reinstate the black grouse to their former haunts. Voicing that general sentiment in 1845, an anonymous commentator asked 'Why do not the noblemen and country gentlemen of England, who take a pride in the manorial accessories and park-like appendages to their halls and castles, more generally introduce this magnificent bird to their ancestral demesnes?'. The noblemen and country gentlemen of England responded.

Despite the fact that some estates persecuted black grouse in favour of the more 'valuable' reds, gamekeepers in the southern uplands were well aware of the benefits that the birds brought to sporting tenants and landowners. In some areas, particularly in Galloway and the Borders, black grouse had come to be a major sporting attraction, and in the absence of large quantities of red grouse, estates with good black grouse numbers were involved in the lucrative practice of preserving birds for shooting. With commendable foresight, keepers and estate managers understood the advantages of refreshing bloodlines and preventing genetic stagnation amongst breeding birds. Eggs were routinely gathered from beneath greyhens, placed in crates and carried by train to be swapped between keepers and estates on either side of the country.

This creeping sense of managerial gamekeeping was gradually extending to traditionally wild and independent game birds. As gamekeeping evolved, more and more knowledge became available to moorland managers, and it seemed like it was becoming possible to care for grouse in a far more active sense than ever before. The inquisitive minds which had pulled pheasants to pieces and put them back together as the ultimate in mass produced sporting targets began to tinker with new ways of working with red and black grouse. The essential principles of moorland management were quickly grasped to maximise the output of existing grouse populations, but that was not enough. Estates wanted to show birds that they may not have had for generations, and starting a new population is quite different from improving an existing one. Landowners in the south of England wanted black grouse on their estates, and historical evidence tantalisingly showed how they had once been abundant. Experimentation in the form of privately-funded translocation projects for black and red grouse started to spring up.

Many of these early projects were initially founded on the assumption that black grouse were similar enough in habit and diet to pheasants for artificial breeding and releasing to guarantee success. As lessons were learned and a strong vein of failure began to run through their results, enthusiasm waned. Captive birds and eggs were shipped around the country in the hope that they might mix in for some nice variety in shooting drives from Norfolk to Southampton, but few birds ever survived more than a year or two.

At the request of Prince Albert, birds were sent from the Drumlanrig estate in Dumfriesshire to Bagshot Heath in Surrey in 1843, although history does not relate how quickly this project folded. Other reintroduction projects in Hampshire, Lincolnshire, Northern Ireland and the Sandringham Estate in Norfolk also fell by the wayside. The British Medical Journal even mentions

a move to ship black grouse eggs to Australia in 1862, although sadly the outcome of this ambitious venture was never documented.

It seems that science and behavioural biology were not being fully exploited. Naturalists and historians had known about the key components of a black grouse's diet for centuries, and many saw how easy it was to successfully hatch eggs. As a devoted naturalist and sportsman, George Morant was amongst the first to explore the potential of keepering black grouse, and he eagerly wrote in 1875 that young black grouse are 'more easily reared tame than pheasants, being much less susceptible to cold and damp, and thriving on exactly the same food, particularly ants' eggs'. However, linking black grouse management with that of pheasants was an unfortunate comparison. Even Morant's early experiences were rife with failure and setbacks.

When he succeeded in rearing nineteen chicks under a greyhen, Morant was thrilled. All was going well until mid-August, when the cock birds had started to turn black. A cat attacked the brood and killed six poults. Morant placed the survivors into a wire 'pheasantry', whereupon they all died within a few weeks. Frustrated but not beaten, he later wrote that '*it would appear that* [black grouse] *do not bear confinement, when young at any rate*'. He later saved an adult blackcock from the approaches of a falcon, and was delighted and confused to find that it survived for months in a similar cage to that which had caused the chicks to sicken and die.

Little did he realise what a complex science he was dabbling in. With

a touchingly misplaced confidence in the advancements of human science, Morant closed his account by saying *'we have but little doubt that* [black grouse] *could be kept when their management was understood'.* Thirty five years later, Hugh Gladstone remarked that *'hand rearing blackgame, so far as my experience goes, is not satisfactory, and the experiment has been tried for many years... with indifferent success'.* The failures were tantalising, particularly since success seemed to be just out of reach.

Here and there, individual birds were kept as pets, and the celebrated naturalist and artist J.G. Millais gives an excellent description of a blackcock which was hand-reared by a friend of his. The bird became extremely tame and enjoyed being taken for walks around the garden while perched upon his master's hat. Millais's writing is filled with charming anthropomorphic language, and there is some tragic humour in his description of the bird's untimely death. He writes:

> *'One summer evening, a strange gutter-bred mongrel, of an unsympathetic nature and loose principles, got into my friend's garden by chance, when of course the unsophisticated child of the forest went to make friends with the vagrant, as was his wont with all newcomers. But the cur either misconstrued his motives, or imagined he was too good and pure a thing for this wicked world, and so promptly sent him on a journey to the next, where we hope his confidences were not misplaced'.*

Other accounts survive of more or less domesticated black grouse, but while the art of rearing many grouse species in captivity has advanced in leaps and bounds over the past century, turning hand-reared birds into a viable population of wild ones still carries with it major problems. Some experts are beginning to wonder if it can actually be done, while others appear to pass off the practice as hardly worth bothering with.

The past ten years have seen the beginnings of a major new conservation project for black grouse on the Isle of Arran. In line with the rest of the country, black grouse on Arran have seen years of terrific boom and bust. By the early nineteenth century, Arran was being used as a private sporting estate by the Duke of Hamilton. Under that typical early Victorian management, it was observed in 1838 that *'red deer are becoming more numerous and tenants can vouch for the amazing increase in black game'.*

Birds were shot on this traditional stronghold for more than a century before creeping declines started to bite. By the early 1960s, they had almost vanished altogether. Unlike on the mainland, where populations were temporarily buoyed by the advent of commercial forestry, black grouse had sunk below a retrievable threshold by the time the moors began to be ploughed up for pines. They withered and died away. The western coast of Arran is just three miles from the Kintyre peninsula, and individual birds were spotted after having made the crossing until around the year 2000, when the last greyhen was seen in a remote area of moorland high off in the hills.

In response to what had become the effective local extinction of black grouse on the island, residents from a variety of backgrounds came together to work on regenerating appropriate habitats, looking forward to a time when they could reintroduce birds to Arran. Reintroduction of black grouse has become something of a bête noir amongst conservation groups, and very few even consider the task at all. Volunteers on Arran were frustrated by the fact that the coordinating body for black grouse conservation in Britain is actively discouraging reintroduction projects on the grounds that none has ever proved sustainable in the long term. The position is galling for the volunteers on Arran because, as an island, birds would naturally struggle to return in reasonable numbers without having their ferry tickets paid for them. They set to work regardless.

It seems sensible enough for the governing European guidelines to stipulate that, in order to release black grouse into a habitat in which they have become extinct, the reasons for that extinction must first be addressed and corrected. Without that basic foundation, even the most successful and technically savvy project is bound to end up in failure. However, once the appropriate habitat is in place, there is no reason why experimentation should not be encouraged. On Arran, tremendous pains were taken to re-establish an appropriate environment for black grouse, and the island now makes up for its comparatively small size with the quality and abundance of its suitable habitat.

For the volunteers at the Arran Black Grouse Group, failure has loomed long and large over their project. When I travelled over the Firth of Clyde to find out more about their endeavours, I was greeted by some of the people who have helped put together one of the most positive and promising black grouse

conservation experiments in the country. A founding member of the group met me in the leafy grounds of Brodick Castle on the island's east coast, and I followed his pickup to a stand of A-frame pens mounted in a small uncut meadow beneath the shattered peak of Goatfell.

I was proudly shown the first of that year's recruits; a clutch of seven speckled chicks raised by a bantam. She clucked through the long grass while the ten day old black grouse crowded along the rough pine backboards, pecking at flies and bluebottles as they landed in the sun. As we talked in the hot afternoon, it was hard to imagine the disasters the volunteers have been through since the group was founded. The little birds seemed to be so full of promise as they stretched their odd, downy trousers in the sunlight and one ducked its head winsomely for shade beneath a buttercup.

On Arran, it has been a long and tortuous road, largely because theirs are some of the first modern attempts to reintroduce black grouse, and the existing store of knowledge surrounding how it can be done simply does not exist. Relying on Victorian accounts of rearing and releasing black grouse certainly provides examples for how not to go about the practice, but the few projects scattered across the country are working in comparative darkness, striving

through new theories and trial and error to come up with a sustainable solution to the problems of reintroduction.

The volunteers on Arran quickly encountered a major stumbling block which, until now, has played a significant part in the failure of many other reintroduction projects. With the experience and accumulated knowledge of generations of ornithologists and bird fanciers, we have learned how to keep and breed black grouse in captivity, but the next step is where complications arise. Releasing hand-reared poults into the wild seems to bring disaster. Despite concerted efforts over the past two hundred years of man's sporting relationship with both red grouse and black grouse, few attempts to artificially breed and release either species have shown any fruit whatsoever. Of 14 reintroduction projects across Europe, the British black grouse BAP (biodiversity action planners) know of only four which resulted in breeding birds, and none in which breeding was shown to be sustainable.

The fact that both red and black grouse rejected man's initial attempts to breed and release them meant that many well-meaning research projects were nipped in the bud by a belief that failure was always inevitable. When the first attempts were made to reintroduce black grouse to areas where they were previously found, the projects were exercises in Victorian conservational enterprise. Like the move to ship black grouse eggs to Australia, many of these projects carried with them the beautifully simplistic determination which was characteristic of British Imperial endeavour. In time, these attempts dwindled into a diminishing series of failures, attempted only by those with enough money to fritter away on doomed hobbies. It was only when black grouse began to show serious signs of becoming extinct in Britain that this centuries old riddle was approached again.

Anecdotally, the reasons behind the failures to breed and release black grouse were so mysterious that they seemed to go beyond the possibility of resolution. Healthy poults grew fat in release pens, but being prone to disease and infection, many died even after being released. Infuriatingly, the dead bodies were shown to be filled with nutritious natural vegetation, but the birds themselves had obviously died of starvation. We now understand a tremendous amount more about infection, and it seems that many of these poults were dying of common avian diseases, but there are also some more complicated reasons for failure. Intestinal development operates on a 'use it or lose it' basis for many grouse species, and unless grouse are taught to digest poor quality roughage as young birds, they will never develop the digestive efficiency to make it in the wild. We now understand that hand-reared black grouse chicks need a carefully-timed switch in their diet from protein to roughage, and we are better than ever at preparing them for a life of poor quality vegetation, but perfecting the process is tricky and takes some careful planning.

Black grouse eggs and chicks are available from a small handful of breeders in Britain, but supply is necessarily limited to a small and experimental demand. It has been suggested that large quantities of available Scandinavian eggs could be used for reintroduction projects in Britain, but since the British black grouse belongs to its own race, mixing bloodlines with others from abroad is not ideal from the purist's perspective. There is some evidence to suggest that Scandinavian black grouse were brought over during the nineteenth and early twentieth centuries to boost or supplement British birds, and *tetrao tetrix britannicus* probably received an influx of foreign genetic material long before the significance of mixing races was even understood.

As it stands, a heavily-diluted version of our native race is being maintained by a few breeders up and down the country, and many of the birds used in high profile re-introduction projects in Britain have actually come from pure Scandinavian stock. With a meagre supply and demand for birds, British black grouse reintroduction projects always need to begin on a relatively small scale.

Several projects focus on producing their own breeding stocks, but the financial cost of these ventures push many to breaking point. With numbers of released birds diminished by sickness and death, the following step towards reconstructing healthy black grouse populations is often heightened in difficulty beyond a tolerable level.

As the keepers of the nineteenth century had discovered, black grouse can be extremely rangy birds. Unlike their essentially sedentary red cousins, black grouse will wander far and wide across large areas of countryside. Young greyhens disperse several miles in their first autumn, and it would seem that a seasonal desire to wander is hardwired into black grouse psychology. The attempt to release black grouse into Northern Ireland in 1839 describes precisely the same problems experienced by modern reintroduction projects up and down the country; namely that within hours of release, the birds simply vanish. In that case, individual birds were found months later, dozens of miles away from their original release sites.

When volunteers on the Isle of Arran released 40 first year poults in the autumn of 2009, they watched in dismay as all the birds burst into the air and disappeared. One greyhen was seen to set her sights on the distant coast of Ayrshire, buzzing her wings until she vanished out of sight. The majority of birds returned to the release pens over the next 24 hours, and the greyhen eventually returned from the mainland, but keeping birds together for extended periods is tricky, particularly away from a small island with natural boundaries.

Many released birds are killed by predators within their first few days of freedom, but some black grouse have been found to move more than twenty miles away from their release sites over the course of a few weeks. Many reintroduction projects are sensibly carried out on well-managed moorland in which predation is not a real problem. Few estates in this country can guarantee a vermin-free environment for a radius of twenty miles, and as the birds disperse, they move away from the safety of their release sites to the dangers of the modern world.

Average survival rates for young black grouse in the wild are fairly bleak. More than 60 percent will die in their first year, and that figure would naturally be far lower in hand-reared birds. They would not acquire the cautious savoir faire of their parents and would blunder into dangerous situations like drunken battery hens. Anecdotally, most of the diminished percentage of birds which survive the process of being hand-reared are cut down by predators in their first few weeks.

For the small number that survive their fiery introduction to the wild, other serious problems soon emerge. As the seasons revolve and hormonal instincts begin to make themselves known, black grouse alter their behaviour, searching for other birds prior to the mating season. In an environment where there is no native population of black grouse, released birds, particularly greyhens, will find themselves dispersing over tremendous distances in search of new lek sites and breeding grounds in the autumn and early spring. The movement will be exacerbated by the fact that they will not be finding the mates that they are looking for, and they will push further and further afield.

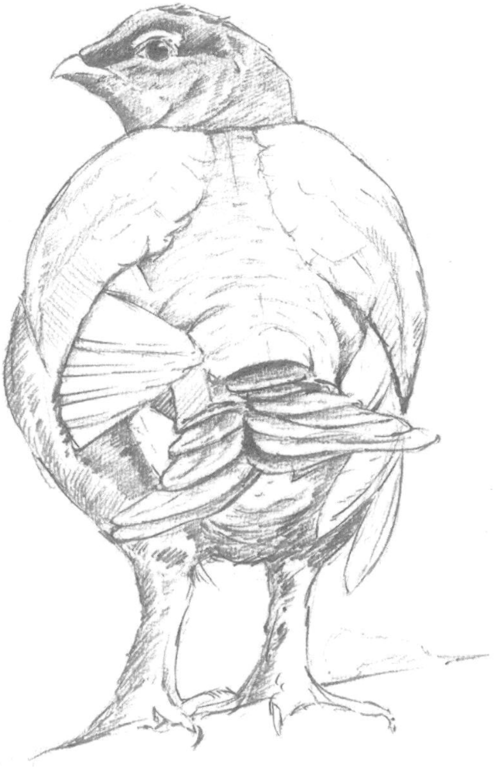

In many cases, breeding becomes a geographical impossibility because birds have finally moved so far apart that they simply cannot find one another. Even if a lek is established in these cases, it is difficult to sustain.

Research has shown that black grouse populations are buoyed by a constant and widespread mixture of bloodlines. On the whole, blackcock are largely sedentary, seldom moving far from the lek at which they were conceived. By comparison, greyhens are predisposed to range long distances from the place of their birth, preventing inbreeding and maintaining a healthy mixture of genetic material. Each autumn, greyhens move far away from their increasingly hormonal brothers, settling in new areas in time for the lekking season. An isolated lek will lose all of its young greyhens every year and receive no replacements, so as a result, half a dozen black and white birds displaying on a cold hillside has to be part of a much larger network.

Lekking behaviour is a massive and interlinking system of genetic exchange, and just as my single blackcock did not make a lek, so one lek does not make a population. Leks work in conjunction with one another, and despite the apparent formality of the behaviour, it can be very flexible and erratic. Lekking is a system which allows greyhens to move between families to prevent genetic stagnation, and which creates a detailed and complex system of tribal hierarchy between individual cock birds, many of whom will be directly related. Young cocks display regardless of whether or not they

4 weeks

8 weeks

10 months

2 years

will mate so as to improve the size of the lek and attract more females to their older brothers and half brothers. At the same time, much older birds who appear to have retired from the process will 'pop in' now and again to keep an eye on what is going on. There is an entire world of research just waiting to be carried out on precisely what is happening when black grouse gather to lek, and until we know some important answers, black grouse conservation is effectively feeling its way in the dark.

The sustainability of reintroduction projects is wholly dependent upon understanding lek behaviour. Unless a number of different and interlinking leks can be quickly established, the reintroduction project will simply become a matter of releasing poults year after year like pheasants, making no real steps towards being able to allow nature to take its course. Dispersing greyhens from one lek need to be able to find other viable leks elsewhere, and if this is not possible, the process of reintroduction will never take off. Thanks to some excellent research carried out in the Peak District, we now know that releasing birds at the start of the lekking season is a much better way to ensure that they stay put. It is now possible to keep birds together to form an artificial but coherent population for longer than ever before, but unravelling the secret world of lekking and lek sites is the next vital step towards making reintroduction a viable practice.

Black grouse lekking displays are tremendously complicated affairs. Nobody knows precisely why some areas are chosen over others. When birds were re-established in traditional haunts in the North Pennines, they were found to be using precisely the same displaying grounds as their extinct forebears. Accounts exist of a lek site being ploughed during the spring and all of the birds returning to the ruined furrows the following morning as if nothing had happened. It would appear that some spots are just 'lekky', and what turns a stretch of grass into a lek site is concealed from the human eye. In Scandinavia, blackcock often lek on frozen lakes. In eastern Europe, some birds lek deep in the forest where they cannot see one another. At times it seems as though there are no rules, while at others, the rules appear to be utterly inflexible. Some researchers believe that the birds seek a spot where the natural acoustics bring out the best in their bubbling calls, and that was a theory I became quite interested in.

When I travelled up to Aviemore to see a capercaillie lek in the spring of 2010, I was not only horrified by the sheer scale of those feathery dinosaurs, but was also fascinated to hear that much of their ritualised communication takes place at a frequency that is well below human hearing. Asking whether or not blackcock make similar inaudible sounds at lek, I found that no known research has been carried out in that area. Some leks take place in natural amphitheatres where natural sound is magnified and concentrated, and these locations could lend credibility to the idea that sound is very important, but without further research, we simply cannot know for sure.

In his second year, my lone blackcock entered March without a greyhen after his first year partner was killed by a buzzard on a snowy afternoon between Christmas and New Year. In her absence, he lekked alone on his former lek site for several days before deciding that he was making no progress. Over the next fortnight, he began to lek further and further away from his original site, gradually moving until he was almost a mile to the west, along a ridge of wet ground. After his displays every morning, he would return to his usual patch and spend the day feeding and slouching around.

In the first week of April, he returned to his lek site and did not move again that season. He had found a greyhen some distance away and had brought her back to his lek site. Why he should have done this is a mystery, and it has no real precedent other than the fact that for some reason, he preferred to lek on one patch only. Black grouse in extremely diminished populations like those on my family's farm are known to behave differently from those in well populated areas, but this bird's actions illustrate the flexibility of behaviour which many regard as set in stone.

In some cases, it seems that greyhens have total control over the blackcock's lekking behaviour, and it is not uncommon to see a single blackcock chasing small packs of greyhens to display to them as they move around the land. This is particularly common early in the lekking season, before structured and formalised behaviour begins to take over, but I have seen mating take place on these improvised leks, and there is no reason why greyhens could not be serviced on their own terms. It is important to remember that the classic formula in which stationary blackcock draw in mobile greyhens to breed is not strictly observed, and there are a thousand variations along this general theme.

The fact that we do no not know precisely what is happening at a lek is a major problem, and it is all too easy to look at a collection of displaying blackcock and assume that it must represent a healthy population. In reality, the health of a population of black grouse must be equally measured by the numbers of greyhens visiting the lek, but the silent brown birds are so much harder to count than their bombastic counterparts.

Some researchers are quite offhand about looking in detail at lek sites, explaining that blackcock will readily lek almost anywhere. This is certainly true, and having been shown photographs of five blackcock lekking on the roof of a log cabin in Scandinavia, it would be hard to deny it, but blackcock are so conspicuous at lek that it is easy to forget about the almost invisible but equally important greyhens. If they don't like where the blackcock are displaying, they will be very unlikely to visit, and given that they are also much more sensitive to human disturbance, their criteria for choosing a good mating ground is quite different to that of a blackcock. Conspicuous leks taking place in unusual places may well draw in other blackcock to compete, but the importance of the greyhen's lekking behaviour is frequently forgotten in favour of a bias towards the iconic and highly visible blackcock.

Many bird watchers have inadvertently destroyed lek sites believing that, because the blackcock did not mind them creeping close in, they were not disturbing the reproductive processes, never realising that their intrusion had scared away the invisible greyhens. The increasing fad for larger and larger tripod-mounted telescopes amongst bird watchers means that few are satisfied with watching a lek from inside a car, and are determined to get out and swing their shiny, 'predator's eye' lenses onto greyhens which are already cautious and jumpy.

It would be a disservice to black grouse conservationists to call lekking behaviour a total mystery, and plenty of excellent research has been carried out on black grouse displays. However, it is important to show that there are several startling gaps in the overall spread of knowledge concerning precisely what is going on when the birds meet, and these gaps may well be inhibiting our attempts to conserve the birds, either through reintroduction or habitat improvement.

Having seen the work of the Arran Black Grouse Group at first hand, it is clear that passion and determination to succeed is by no means in short supply, but support from some conservation charities has been much harder to come by. The RSPB are known for having little interest in reintroducing black grouse, and they choose to focus their attentions only upon habitat regeneration, a vital part of black grouse conservation. Now and again, official releases are heard to speak in vague terms about the potential for investment in future black grouse reintroduction projects, but having spoken to various volunteers and officials in that Society, many are either reluctant to discuss the prospect or have no knowledge that it could even be possible. As a result, they are missing out on some fascinating practical research which is now being carried out independently by small conservation groups like that on Arran. In many

areas across the country, reintroduction is effectively the only possible means of reinstating black grouse numbers. How birds would ever return to the west country and Hampshire without artificial releases is a total mystery, and to stubbornly focus solely upon an impossible strategy of nationwide habitat management without considering the possibility of active reintroduction is naive and short-sighted.

The RSPB are relatively elusive on why they will not support existing reintroduction projects, and despite my repeated attempts to discuss the subject with them during research for this project, I have always been met with the same statement; that the RSPB is concentrating its efforts on trying to promote habitat improvements for the species, in areas where it already occurs, in order to stop their decline. As a major weight in the world of British conservation, the RSPB hold a serious sway in discussions about black grouse, and their apparent failure to promote, study or support existing black grouse reintroduction projects is without a doubt causing harm to conservation strategies nationwide. Some cynical observers have remarked that the process of releasing gamebirds into the wild has become so sullied by sporting shooting that a major conservation charity finds the entire process unpalatable. In addition, if black grouse do continue to decline, the shooting community is a convenient scapegoat.

In truth, reintroduction is really starting to look like a workable solution to black grouse decline. Thanks to research in Derbyshire and the Peak District, we understand the vital cornerstones upon which the process needs to be founded, and it could be that it is simply a matter of time before real progress will be made. However, for real success, the casual assumption that black grouse are just like other gamebirds needs to be totally abandoned.

Pheasants and partridges can be easily released in large quantities to form cohesive and long-lasting populations which ultimately become wild. These quick results simply do not apply to black grouse. Their reintroduction needs a committed application of time and money over several years before similar results can be seen, and the fact that it has not yet succeeded in any major way has always been down to the fact that projects like these are extremely difficult to sustain for an appropriate timescale. A landowner with quality habitat and sufficiently deep pockets could be looking at a self-sustaining population of black grouse within ten years of gradual and systematic release. It is a tall order, but with the future of these iconic birds hanging in the balance, there is no doubt that it is a price worth paying, particularly since there is no evidence to suggest that it is a process that cannot be carried out alongside existing releases of partridges or pheasants, or the management of red grouse.

It may even be that reintroduction in an area like Galloway could have really positive effects on the surviving vestiges of the local population. Although releasing birds to supplement an existing population is not technically 'reintroduction', Galloway's population of black grouse is so scant as to be almost non-existent. In order to combat the inevitable and destructive process of inbreeding in a small population, it could be that an area with a failing population of birds could really benefit from a pseudo-reintroduction/release project.

Even if such a project fails to re-establish defunct leks, a fresh influx of blood and genetic material could well reinvigorate a native population and add fire to the bellies of a directionless and disparate community of closely-related birds. In addition, in an area where the remains of an existing system of leks and breeding grounds is still visible, releasing poults into a dwindling population could cut several corners and simplify the trickiest aspects of reintroduction from scratch.

A basic variation on the theme of reintroduction is the practice of translocation, in which adult birds are captured and moved to the outer limits of existing black grouse ranges. Blackcock are the particular target for these schemes, given that they have less of a natural inclination to wander from their home lek sites and that establishing new leks will draw in greyhens naturally from the surrounding area. As black grouse continue to decline, many of their former strongholds become more and more isolated. It is vital to keep these pockets of birds linked together, and translocation is an excellent way of opening corridors between groups of existing birds.

The Game and Wildlife Conservancy Trust in the North Pennines is currently working not only to consolidate the populations that they already have, but to expand ranges by translocation and ensure that birds do not become isolated and unable to move between groups. Translocation is an excellent weapon in the fight against black grouse population collapse, but, like all attempts to reverse the decline in British black grouse populations, it is limited by its dependence upon existing and well-keepered habitats.

Despite promising signs for reintroduction and translocation, there is a potentially catastrophic complication waiting in the wings. It could soon become harder and harder to conduct privately-funded reintroduction projects thanks to new webs of bureaucracy proposed by government-funded conservation specialists. These 'experts' considered the possibility in 2010 that black grouse should be included on a list of species such as mink, porcupines and parakeets, making it illegal to release them into the wild. Releasing black grouse would still be possible, but it would be subject to close legal regulation. This is apparently in response to the non-existent risk which black grouse reintroduction schemes currently pose to the biosecurity of the nation.

There is clearly no logic or purpose behind this suggestion other than to take black grouse out of the hands of private reintroduction projects, so that centralised conservation charities can hold a monolithic mandate on the future of these birds. The motives behind this proposal are unclear, but for a process that simply needs to be worked out through trial and error, it could spell total disaster. Privately-funded conservation projects are at the heart of all country sports, and this minute legal alteration could put black grouse out of the hands of the people best suited to help them.

It may be that reintroduction will become an indispensable method for returning black grouse to their former haunts, but for now, it is underexplored

and labelled as wasteful and directionless. It could be that, barring legal intrusion, I will one day be able to reintroduce black grouse on my family's farm, but remembering the mantra of reintroduction, it would be pointless without proper habitat creation and management.

PART ELEVEN

Conclusion

Looking to the future

And so here we are. The British countryside evolves and changes with every passing day. Forests are being felled and planted as I write, and every new spring meets a country that is without a doubt 'on the move'. Recent trends in farming and agricultural policy have meant that grants are increasingly available for country people to turn back the clock to a less intensive age, and while rural progress comes on in leaps and bounds every year, a fair proportion of change is regressive. It is a swirling mixture of old and new, and despite the fact that the past fifty years has seen a decline of many major British bird species, dedicated work by farmers and conservationists is not only finding new ways to protect struggling species but looks equally at turning back to a more traditional way of using the land.

Like it or loathe it, tourism is becoming one of Britain's most important industries. Despite the fact that maintaining meadow land is uneconomical, grants are available to make the flowers pay. We do not attract visitors to the nation to see modern farming techniques; fifty acre fields of oilseed rape or a thousand dairy cows in a shed. The romantic view is the old view; paddocks of oxeye daisies and Hereford cows flicking their tails under a sprawling oak tree. These are the typical British scenes seared year after year into miles of foreign camera film, but subsidised beauty is a temperamental thing. Just as it doesn't take long to mow a meadow and plough it for crops, so the rolling moorlands of upland Britain can be easily spoiled.

The late twentieth century saw thousands of acres of traditional hill country vanish overnight underneath a carpet of trees, solely because economics determined that there were better ways of using the land. The fact that agri-environmental schemes are drawing a great deal of interest at the moment does not mean that they are the solution to Britain's overall decline in biodiversity. The recent global financial crisis and the ensuing economic chaos saw the risk of dramatic cuts to conservation grants and charities. Had they been followed through as many gloomy observers predicted, British conservation could have been put back by decades. Grants are not a reliable enough framework upon which to base the future of a struggling species, and it is time that we started to look elsewhere.

Black grouse have declined because they did not pay their own way. When new ways of using wet, rough and unprofitable land appeared, black grouse vanished because when it came to choosing between having money and having birds, landowners hardly needed to think twice. Today, they can largely be found on land that is so remote and poor that not even foresters would consider developing it.

Each step taken in habitat change has been governed by human economics, and although many grants are now available to gear land use towards these birds, habitat regeneration is essentially passive. Grants may enable suitable habitat to be installed, but history has shown that black grouse need active help if they are to prosper. Foxes and crows need to be controlled; woods need to be worked using gentle and rotational cycles and more research is needed into raptor predation and poult reintroduction. This all not only needs money but depends equally on time and work, which is hard to come by in the name of a bird that simply looks pretty and puts on a nice display in the spring. What the landowners of Britain need to realise is the fact that black grouse are far more than that.

Two centuries of sporting shooting have sealed the preservation of red grouse for generations to come. Fantastic quantities of money are spent every year on ensuring that red grouse prosper, and despite stubbornly pessimistic

press releases by some anti-shooting organisations, their core habitats go from strength to strength. England's greatest stronghold of black grouse only exists because it is clinging onto the coat tails of the red grouse. Teesdale and Weardale have some of the finest grouse moors in the country, and the carefully-managed patchwork of purples and greens is one of the nation's natural wonders. Foxes and crows are effectively non-existent, and in that environment, black grouse survive in the same way as do curlews and lapwings; they complete the picture, but only as a finishing touch. The money is not really being spent on them, and they benefit from the investments largely because they do no harm. Obviously, landowners in the North Pennines have a great affection for black grouse, but their sliding decline throughout the twentieth century has left the birds as an object of pity.

It followed simple logic that when black grouse numbers fell below an acceptable threshold that a voluntary moratorium on shooting them was put in place, but what we now assume is that the birds have effectively become protected. It is a disastrous misconception, because the high-paced fuel of shooting economics is now being increasingly geared away from the birds.

Many keepers I have spoken to have referred to the fact that estates view managing red grouse as work and black grouse as a sort of a hobby. Black grouse are losing their status as gamebirds altogether, and every incremental shift away from the school of thought which held them in high esteem as a valuable sporting commodity is another nail in their coffin.

Some argue that, since a voluntary moratorium on shooting black grouse is in place, it makes sense to offer them full legal protection. This is an unreasonable position because it implies that shooting continues to be a key cause of black grouse decline. Tiny numbers of greyhens are shot when

they are mistaken for red grouse or hen pheasants, and during some drives a brace or two of blackcock are deliberately taken when a harvestable surplus has presented itself, but the idea that the birds need legal protection from a ravenous and uncontrollable shooting community is utter nonsense. A ban on shooting capercaillie was introduced in 2001, and numbers continued to decline for the next decade regardless.

Having seen greyhens rising with red grouse on a moor in the Scottish Borders, I can see how the two might be confused in bad light and a cold wind, and I have some sympathy for the unfortunate and usually red-faced guns who are invariably forced to stump up a penalty for their mistake. It is easy to get hung up on these mistakes, and the RSPB have been known to cause a major fuss over individual birds killed in error during grouse shoots. According to the GWCT, only around three per cent of black grouse killed each year are shot, and it would not be hard to imagine that a similar percentage is killed as a result of being hit by cars. Having found a half moulted blackcock lying dead in a drainage ditch by M74 between Moffat and Abington during the summer of 2010, I asked around for more information on roads as a hazard for black grouse. It seems that several have been killed while lekking on roads in the North Pennines, and recent accounts survive of similarly depressing road traffic accidents across the Scottish Borders and into the Highlands. If we put shooting alongside these other accidental deaths, they start to be put into perspective.

No sportsman would ever knowingly shoot a black grouse unless he was given specific instructions to do so from the shoot's organiser, and in turn, no shoot organiser would give those instructions without a sound knowledge of local populations. The few birds deliberately shot each year serve an important purpose by keeping their status as game birds alive. Legal protection would make no short-term difference to black grouse numbers whatsoever, and the possible long term effects of such a move could be disastrous. Experience has shown that once a bird becomes protected, it never returns to the quarry list, so a move to protect black grouse would be as final as it would be fatal.

Although the RSPB and their associates have invested a great deal of time and money into black grouse conservation, their work is meaningless in isolation. Every project they fund may well boost our understanding of black grouse habitat and biology, but conserving birds in small reserves is a hopeless exercise. What is more, the RSPB's failure to connect with sporting landowners devalues their research by limiting the area in which the results can be implemented.

Black grouse need large, interlinking ranges if they are to keep bloodlines and gene pools alive, and the sort of scale they depend upon can only be offered by the collaboration of large private landowners, particularly those responsible for interlinking and well-keepered shoots. RSPB reserves dot the country here and there, but nowhere do they offer the massive, large scale ranges which will ultimately preserve black grouse for the long term. Gamekeepers are responsible for managing an area of Britain that is thirteen times larger than all government-funded nature reserves combined. As a sport, shooting holds the future of British wildlife in its hands to a far greater extent than any conservation charity, thanks if nothing else to the scale of land it manages.

The RSPB need to see a return on their investments, and they charge birdwatchers money to take guided tours around lek sites throughout the spring. Conservation charities have every right to rebrand black grouse as an exotic novelty; nobody owns the birds and they lend themselves to continuous reinterpretation. With companies in Scandinavia charging up to £1,500 for a week photographing capercaillie and black grouse at lek, some British photographers are fast catching on to the fact that black grouse can bring in serious money. Some tour companies are starting to be able to charge similar prices in the Cairngorms National Park, and the fast-growing world of photographic tourism is expanding to claim good money from black grouse. By increments, black grouse are starting to sustain themselves as a tourist novelty, but their real potential is as a game bird.

Visiting the GWCT trust in their office high up on the hills above Barnard Castle, I spoke to Dr. Phil Warren, one of the country's foremost black grouse conservationists. As we talked, lapwings whirled over the bog outside the house, and we came at last to the future of black grouse in Britain. Unlike so many conservationists, Dr. Warren sees a great deal of light at the end of the tunnel for the birds. In 2007, they were managed well enough to allow a shootable surplus in the dales. The GCWT is not merely preserving black grouse 'for people, for birds, forever' like the RSPB, but is working

Meadow pipit

towards reinstalling the birds as a viable game species. It can be done, but a predisposition towards failure and a reluctance to begin long-term projects are some of the key reasons why work is not being put in. A century ago, sporting commentators remarked that 'there are many moors in the kingdom upon which the black grouse might be exploited' . There are certainly fewer today, but the potential remains. The key word in the remark is 'exploited'; it carries with it negative connotations, but there can be no doubt that we need to 'use or lose' black grouse.

Red grouse have risen above the uncertainty of agri-environmental schemes because they generate a sustainable source of income, or at least an income which offsets the outlay to a manageable extent. Black grouse faded into obscurity too long ago for many modern guns to remember them, and so they are now an entertaining but ultimately valueless side show. Changing our approach to land management and remembering the challenging sport offered by black grouse throughout the nineteenth and twentieth centuries, it is still possible to stage a major renaissance in moorland shooting.

Research has shown that in northern England and in the central Highlands, black grouse centre their populations on the fringes of land managed to the benefit of red grouse. These areas have established reputations as fine sporting venues, and despite meteorological hiccups, black grouse are relatively safe for the time being. Here and there, individual estates allow guns to shoot a handful of birds on a good year, but even if populations were to return to their former numbers, black grouse would always be playing second fiddle. The areas of real potential are away from the big grouse moors.

The traditional notion of the black grouse as a bird of the heather moorland is correct, but the often forgotten fact is that they are also happy to live in any number of other habitats. So much black grouse conservation is carried out

in and around major red grouse moors by pro-shooting charities such as the GWCT that the misleading impression is that heather is the paramount key to success for black grouse. There is no doubt that it is important to complete the birds' annual diet, but several populations manage very well with hardly any of the purple undergrowth.

Maybe charities like the GWCT should be focusing their black grouse conservation work away from big grouse moors to illustrate the fact that more or less any upland farm in the country can be made to provide quality habitat for black grouse. By doing so, they could not only learn about black grouse in 'the real world' of vermin and agriculture where decline is at its most dramatic, but they would also demonstrate the stunning potential for growth and regeneration in regions where, year by year, populations continue to vanish forever.

Southern Scotland, Cumbria and North Wales once held richly-deserved reputations as quality sporting destinations. These areas have been hardest hit by changes in land use, and dozens of good moorland shoots have come to pieces over the past century. The fact that red grouse are almost absent while tiny populations of black grouse still survive means that these localised remnants have an extraordinary sporting potential. Free from the bias towards red grouse, black grouse could and should be preserved and restored to allow an old form of shooting to resume. Every year new shooting syndicates are being formed and shooting is the fastest-growing sport in the nation. Rather than spilling reared pheasants across the uplands, it is perfectly possible to work on black grouse to provide a rare opportunity for some unique sport.

Time is certainly a factor, particularly since black grouse breeding cycles are comparatively slow, but a sensible and patient landowner is more than capable of managing his property to attract financial dividends from the shooting community. By taking advantage of existing grants and funding, farmers and landowners can take positive and active steps which will not only pay for themselves, but which will also provide habitat for generations of black grouse in the future. The birds have shown themselves to be sustainably shootable, and there is no reason at all why modern British sportsmen should not work towards producing a harvestable surplus of the birds every year, particularly if they can be managed alongside other gamebirds.

In Scandinavia and Eastern Europe, where black grouse are abundant, large quantities of money are spent each year on shooting black grouse. In Belorussia, birds can be shot over pointers for around fifty pounds a head, and vast areas of suitable habitat are maintained for the purposes of supporting a lucrative surplus of cock birds. In Lapland and Sweden, European clients pay more than £150 to shoot single birds at lek sites with centrefire rifles.

Although the prospect of shooting a bird on the ground is now unpalatable to British sportsmen, perhaps we should acknowledge a demand from European hunters who want to shoot a trophy blackcock in full display plumage. Open seasons are notoriously inflexible in Britain and it is naive to publicly suggest the extension to the legal shooting season of what has become an endangered species, but hypothetically speaking, it could be that if populations were sufficiently revived, black grouse would benefit from a short window of legal sporting attention in March or early April, before breeding processes become fully active.

I can sense experienced guns grinding their teeth with horror as I write, but the fact is that black grouse face the very real prospect of disappearing altogether, and without serious reinterpretations of sporting protocol, we could risk losing the birds forever. In the same way, just 200 years ago experienced sportsmen curled their lips at the prospect of driven grouse, while today it is revered as the cream of sporting shooting. Tradition is a fine thing and makes British sport unique, but it cannot be allowed to become so inflexible that it stifles change and innovation. The history of game shooting is characterised by change, and we must resist the temptation to think that we cannot improve upon the sport we now enjoy.

If, for example, black grouse numbers were improved and a European style culture of shooting birds at lek was legalised, few British guns would have much interest in the change. However, in one fell swoop, black grouse would start to be able to pay their own way. In the presence of an experienced and responsible stalker, older birds could be selectively and sustainably culled for the benefit of the wider population. For three days hunting black grouse in Lapland, sportsmen are invited to pay more than £1,500; a tempting incentive for British landowners. True, that price is based upon an experience involving cross country skiing and stalking in deep snow, but there is no reason why an imaginative sporting agent could not concoct something equally memorable around the selective culling of blackcock in Great Britain.

Having seen it at first hand, much of South African game hunting is based around the wholly artificial premise of shooting semi-tame animals around feeding stations, yet European and American clients are prepared to spill money all over the practice, financing vital conservation work and ploughing money back into habitat management. British landowners might wrinkle their noses at the very suggestion of similar activities in this country, but in many areas, we need to be aware that make-or-break time is fast approaching for black grouse.

European sportsmen have a great interest in black grouse, and it would not take a great deal of reshuffling and innovation to open up a revived population of British birds to a foreign market, even within our traditional shooting seasons. After the visitors had gone, British landowners would be delighted to support black grouse for another year if they had paid their way, and the birds would earn themselves an economic independence which they sadly lack today.

Encouraging foreign sportsmen could be a stepping stone to restoring black grouse to something approaching their former numbers, and once they return to show themselves as sporting targets for British guns, interest in the birds will no doubt return. Shooting is big business, and there is a distinctly competitive element to modern estate management. If individual estates could offer a half day shooting black grouse once or twice in a season alongside red grouse or partridges, they would gain a real edge over their competitors. Shooting techniques perfected by the 1970s showed that driving black grouse away from their roost woods shortly before the darkening allowed a certain amount of entertaining walked up shooting, but what happened next was real magic.

Once the birds had escaped the beating line, they flew far ahead and marshalled themselves. After a short interval, they began to return to their roost woods, high over the guns and flying like lightning. Sporting journalists have noticed since the birth of 'shooting flying' that blackcocks, once in the air, will seldom deviate their courses, and high birds flying back to roost can offer thrilling sport at the end of a day's shooting. In recent years, duck and woodcock flights have become a fashionable way to end a shoot, and often, these small diversions offer some of the best sport of the day. The opportunity to make use of black grouse in a sporting context certainly exists, and if, for example, this technique was further explored, it could prove to be a real asset for commercial shoots. History has shown that it is a difficult job to get a full day's sport from black grouse, but through a combination of improvised drives and experimental practices, the birds could be brought to add a lucrative spice of variety to a day's commercial grouse or pheasant shooting.

This sense of variety is nothing new to British shooting, but it is something that has clearly declined over the past fifty years. Today, we have a large number of private shooting estates which are becoming increasingly commercial and predicated upon numbers. The Victorians and Edwardians focused on bag sizes as being of social importance; today, it is financial. So many partridges and pheasants are released into the wild every autumn that it is now unusual to shoot anything else. On a normal shoot day, it is perfectly feasible that pheasants and partridges will be the only birds in the bag. Mallard sometimes rise from fed ponds and woodcock appear here and there to fly the flag for truly wild birds, but variety has become effectively extinguished from the British sporting field. A century ago, a gun might have recorded eight or nine different game species on an ordinary day's driven shooting; today, a gun might be happy with four.

While a demand for commercial shooting develops and evolves every year, there is increasingly an argument for the promotion of smaller shoots with a wider remit for conservation. Five times as many pheasants are released into the countryside each year as were in the early 1960s, and the expanding nature of commercial shooting as it stands could well prove to be unsustainable. It is in no way reprehensible to release thousands of pheasants for the sake of large bags, but a trend towards smaller releases and more work on habitat management for wild game species could easily resurrect the lost sense of bag variety, cementing shooting's role as a force for conservation in the eyes of a general public that is keen to pick faults in country sports. Black grouse may never again be the sole object of a day's sport, but along with golden plover, brown and blue hares and ptarmigan, they could seal their future prosperity and provide great pleasure for a gun who has grown tired of seeing the skies blacken with pheasants.

One of the greatest obstacles in restoring black grouse for the sake of shooting is that the existing generation of moorland managers has seen at first hand the tragic collapse of healthy populations. As soon as voluntary bans came in on black grouse shooting, they became strictly followed and personally emotive policies. On several estates where black grouse are present in sufficient numbers to be shot, they continue to be protected because sporting opinion cannot shake off the fear of history repeating itself. Black grouse are now widely perceived as being underdogs, and there is a real possibility that we will lose the birds from the quarry list altogether.

This simple legislative move must not be allowed to happen because it effectively seals the fate of black grouse, cementing them as a tourist's gimmick and restricting their capacity for long-term growth and restoration. It would be irresponsible to advocate an immediate resumption of black grouse shooting as it was, but if we can shake off the associated history which portrays black grouse as a weak and vulnerable bird, we can start to think of new ways of using them to make money. Whether half a dozen birds are shot on an improvised day in October or a single cock is shot at the lek, black grouse can pay for themselves and generate sufficient income to guarantee their future survival. They are truly fantastic birds, and looking at their history in Great Britain, they need to be shot to be fully appreciated. It would be illogical to return black grouse to their former numbers purely to shoot them in large quantities, but sensitively building a harvestable surplus of these birds, along with the associated benefits to other species, would provide a much-needed opportunity to return to the roots of shooting.

In a population of wild animals, there should be no such thing as an individual. It was foolish of me to develop a particular attachment to one blackcock as I did during the course of writing this book, but in my defence, blackcock lend themselves to anthropomorphism. I applied human characteristics to one bird and interpreted its behaviour as a 'personality' which I found amusing. Having seen black grouse across the nation, I can now see that although I thought that my bird was quite the finest in creation, I was actually becoming hooked on black grouse as species. Stepping back to view them as a whole makes one or two things much clearer.

The media occasionally bandies around the popular and misleading sentiment that shooting and conservation are opposites. Urban journalists fill their columns with self-satisfied rhetorical questions such as 'How can you claim to conserve an animal when you want to kill it?' That logic shows an essential failure to understand the concept of wildlife management and grievously misinterprets the motives of the shooting community.

After a wet and unproductive day in the hills above Achnasheen, an old stalker once told me that when he hangs up a stag at the end of a hard stalk, he is not looking at an individual beast, but what he described in his own words as 'a piece of deer'. The implication was that, as a stalker, he was responsible for a single vast 'deer' which took the form of many individual animals. In his mind, stalking a stag was nothing more than pruning a favourite bush. His affection was not for the individual, but for the species, and as a result, he could take pleasure and satisfaction from a situation in which one of his beloved animals was being killed.

When we use his very sensible philosophy to look at black grouse, we see that I shouldn't have got hung up on individual birds as I have done throughout this book. Although the idea of shooting my blackcock makes my hair stand on end with horror, it is very clear that shooting is a sport which provides many of the answers to the serious problems facing black grouse. If I can resurrect my birds to numbers at which they can be shot again, I will feel no qualms about taking to the hills with a shotgun under my arm; indeed, it is a primary motive for all that I have done with this project.

Contrary to the loud-mouthed opinions of ignorant journalists, killing a wild animal is not a victorious act inspired by a desire to destroy and debase. Killing brings with it a variety of emotions, from satisfaction and excitement to sorrow and shame. Most importantly, it can be an extended and logical form of interaction with an animal, providing an intimate and deeply personal opportunity to learn. As a result, game shooting encourages a natural form of 'practical ornithology', in which a human can become physically involved with bird life, rather than merely observing it.

To me, this book would have been incomplete without showing an essential interest in death as a part of life and killing as a form of acquaintanceship. I look forward to the day when I can bring down my first blackcock to feel its feathers and run my fingers over its scaled toes. Killing a bird should give satisfaction borne equally of conquest and exploration, and it follows easily that a true sportsman holds a great affection and fascination for his quarry.

Aside from the grim financial incentives of managing land to benefit black grouse, shooting people have a responsibility for the birds. Although it is clear that shooting was not responsible for their population collapse, country folk are on the verge of losing one of their most unique gamebirds. For thousands of years, man has lived side by side with black grouse and it has been a fascinating and colourful relationship. Shooting people may not have made this gloomy situation as it looms before them, but they need to fix it. Every year, an increasingly urbanised British population asks more and more questions of country sportsmen. The barrier between town and country has never been more pronounced, and there will be no excuses when the shooting community is one day asked why they need to artificially produce massive numbers of pheasants and partridges. The question 'why don't you shoot wild birds anymore?' will be very hard to answer.

It will not be easy to save black grouse, but shooting alone can do it. Every edition of the *Shooting Times* carries that famous quote by King George VI alongside the main banner. 'The wildlife of today is not ours to dispose of as we please. We have it in trust. We must account for it to those who come after'. The nation will lose a valuable asset if black grouse are allowed to vanish, but country sports could lose much more. After all, if there is no longer a place for native gamebirds like black grouse in our countryside, then perhaps there is no longer a place for shooting.

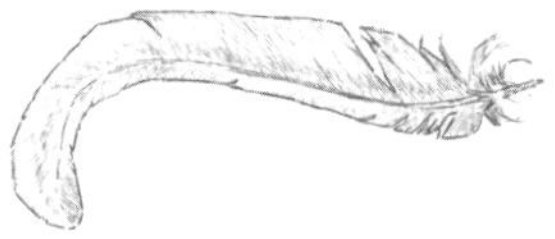

Bibliography

Books

Adams, H.G. (c.1863) *Our Feathered Families: Game and Water Birds.* London, James Hogg & sons.

Anderson, J. (1813) *The Bee, or Literary Weekly Intelligencer* Vol. 14. Edinburgh, Priv. Pub.

Anon. (1834) *Sporting Magazine*, or Monthly Calendar of the Transactions of the Turf, the Chase, and every other diversion interesting to the man of pleasure, enterprise and spirit. Vol. IX, 2nd Series. London, M.A. Pitman.

Anon. (1852) *Blackwood's Edinburgh Magazine.* Vol. 72 July-December. Edinburgh, Blackwood.

Barry, W. (1871) *Moorland and Stream.* London, Slyne & Co.

Beeton, I.M. (1865) *Mrs Beeton's Dictionary of Everyday Cookery.* London, S. Beeton.

Carlisle, G.L. (1983) *Grouse and Gun.* London, Stanley Paul.

Carmichael, A. (2007) *Carmina Gadelica: Hymns and Incantations.* Charleston, Forgotten Books.

Chapman, A. (1990) *Bird Life of the Borders* (1889). Stocksfield, Spreddon Press.

Chapman, A. (1928) *Retrospect: reminiscences and impressions of a hunter-naturalist in three continents 1851-1928.* London, Gurney & Jackson.

Colquhuon, J. (1842) *The moor and the loch* [2nd Ed]. John Murray, London.

Cuvier, G. et al. (1834) *A System of Natural History.* Brattleboro', Peck & Wood.

Dougall, J.D. (1865) *Shooting Simplified, a concise treatise on guns and shooting.* London, R. Hardwicke.

Fraser, Sir H. (1923) *Amid the High Hills.* London, A&C Black Ltd.

Freeman, G.E. and Salvin, F.H. (1859) *Falconry, its claims, history and practice.* London, Longman, Green, Longman & Roberts.

Gladstone, H.S. (1910) *The Birds of Dumfriesshire.* London, Witherby & Co.

Gladstone H.S. (1923) *Notes on the Birds of Dumfriesshire* (a continuation of the birds of Dumfriesshire). Dumfries, D&GNHAS.

Glass, J. [as Ellangowan] (2005) *Outdoor sports in Scotland: their economy and surroundings: deer stalking, grouse shooting, salmon angling, etc. with notes on the natural and sporting history of the animals of the chase,* 1889. Alcester, Read Country Books.

Grey, R. (1871) *The birds of the west of Scotland: including the outer Hebrides, with occasional records of the occurrence of the rarer species throughout Scotland generally.* Edinburgh, T.Murray & Sons.

Hamilton, J.P. (1860) *Reminiscences of an Old Sportsman* Vol. I. London, Longman, Green, Longman & Roberts.

Hawker, Col. P. (1893) *The Diary of Colonel Peter Hawker 1802-1853.* Vol. I. London, Longmans, Green & Co.

Hawker, Col. P. (1859) *Instructions to young sportsmen in all that relates to guns and shooting.* 11th Ed. London, Longman, Brown, Green, Longmans & Roberts.

Hawker, Col. P. (1985) *Colonel Hawker's Shooting Diaries.* Rhyl, Tideline.

Hicks, J. (1855) *Wanderings by the Lochs and Streams of Assynt and the North Highlands of Scotland.* London, Blackwood.

Home, Lord. (1979) *Border Reflections.* London, Collins.

Jackson, A. (1974) *So You Want To Go Shooting.* London, Arlington Books.

Jardine, Sir W. (1844) *The Natural History of Gamebirds.* Edinburgh, W.H. Lizars.

Johnson, T.B. (1819) *The Shooter's Companion.* London, Longman, Hurst, Rees, Orme & Brown.

Knox, A.E. (1850) *Game Birds and Wild Fowl.* London, J.Van Voorst.

Lloyd, L. (1830) *Fieldsports in the North of Europe* [Vol. I]. London, Colburn & Bentley.

MacPherson, H.A. (1897) *A History of Fowling, being an account of the many curious devices by which birds are or have been captured in different parts of the world.* Edinburgh, D.Douglas.

Markland A.B. (1767) *Pteryplegia: or, the art of shooting-flying, a poem.* (3rd Ed.) London, J.Lever.

Marksman (1861) *The Dead Shot, or Sportsman's Complete Guide.* London, Spottiswoode & Co.

Martin, M.A. (1703) *A Description of the Western Isles of Scotland.* London, Andrew Bell.

Maxwell, W.J. (1887) 'The destruction of beasts and birds of prey', given as a lecture and published in *The Transactions and Journal of Proceedings of The*

Dumfriesshire and Galloway Natural History and Antiquarian Society, sessions 1883-1884, 1884-1885 and 1885-1886. Dumfries, Courier & Herald.

McGillivray, W. (1836) *Descriptions of the Rapacious Birds of Great Britain.* Edinburgh, MacLachlan & Stewart Millais, J.G. (1894) *Game Birds and Shooting Sketches: Illustrating the habits, modes of capture, stages of plumage and the hybrids and varieties.* London, Henry Sotheran & Co.

Morant, G.F. (1875) *Game preservers and bird preservers, which are our friends?* London: Longmans, Green & Co.

Mortimer Batten, H. (1923) *Inland Birds: Observations by a Sportsman.* London, Hutchinson & Co.

Neil, W.K. & Black D.H.L. (1966) *The Mantons: Gunmakers.* London, Herbert Jenkins.

Nettleship, J. (1813) *The Trigger, or shooter's pocket guide.* London, Field & Bull.

Nimrod et al. (1845) *The Illustrated Book of Rural Sports.* London, H.G. Bohn.

Oakleigh, T. (1836) *The Oakleigh Shooting Code.* London, J. Ridgeway & sons.

Palmar, C.E. (1968) *Blackgame: Forest Record* No. 66. London, HMSO.

Parker, E. (1954) *The Shooting Week-end Book.* London, Seeley Service.

Rayner, R. (2003) *The Story of the Sporting Gun.* Newton Abbot, David & Charles.

Redpath, S.M. (c.1997) *Birds of Prey and Red Grouse.* London, The Stationery Office.

Rusticus (1849) *The letters of Rusticus on the Natural History of Godalming.* London, J. Van Voorst.

Scott, Sir W. (1830) *A Legend of Montrose.* Boston, SH Parker.

Scott, Sir W. (1834) *Waverley.* Boston, Samuel Parker.

Scott, Sir W. (1855) *Guy Mannering* – Abbotsford Ed. of the Waverley Novels in XII vols [Vol. I]. Philadelphia, Lippincott, Grambo & Co.

Scott, Lord G. (1937) *Grouse Land and the Fringe of the Moor.* London, H.F.&G. Witherby.

Scott Elliot, G.F. (1912) 'Scotch Forestry' – a lecture given on 16.2.1912 and published in *The Transactions and Journal of Proceedings of the Dumfriesshire and Galloway Natural History and Antiquarian Society*, Sessions 1911-1912. Dumfries, Courier & Herald Office.

Simpson, R. (1866) *The Cottars of the Glen.* Glasgow, J. Menzies.

Stanford, J.K. (1963) *Grouse Shooting* – The Shooting Times Library. London, Percival Marshall & Co.

Stuart-Wortley, H.A. (1894) *Grouse, Fur and Feather Series.* London, Longmans, Green & Co.
St John, C. (1893) *The Wild Sports and Natural History of the Highlands.* London, John Murray.
Traill, T.S. [Ed.] (1860) *Encyclopaedia Britannica* 8th Ed. Edinburgh, A&C Black.
Vesey-Fitzgerald B. (1946) *British Game.* London, Collins.
Vincent, Rev. J. (1808) *Fowling; a poem in five books.* London, Cadell & Davies.
Walsh, Dr. J.H. (2008) *Manual of British Rural Sports: The pursuit of wild animals for sport* (1856). Stroud, The History Press.
Watson, A. & Moss, R. (2008) *Grouse.* London, Collins.

Journals, Articles and Periodicals

Anon. (1998) *The Bird That's Killing the Moor* - featured in the *Daily Telegraph*, 1.11.1998 p.25
Anon. (1862) *The British Medical Journal.* ed. WO Markham Vol. I, 1862.
Anon. (1838) *The North British Advertiser* 29.9.1838
Stephen, D. (1965) 'On the Lek' from the *Scottish Field*, October.
Marcstrom (1988) & Tapper (1996). featured in Report of the UK Raptor Working Group. Published Feb. 2000
Wood, R. 'Cattle help black grouse survive' in the *Glasgow Herald*, Saturday, July 10th, 2010.

Online resources and PDFs

UK BAP Reintroduction Position Statement - accessed online at http://www.blackgrouse.info/management/reintroduction.htm on 17.7.2010
Thompson, W. *The Annals and Magazine of Natural History*, Vol. XII (London: R & JE Taylor: 1843)
http://www.blackgrouse.info/advice/publications/BlackGrouseConservation-Guide.pdf
http://www.moorlandassociation.org/black_grouse.asp accessed on 29.7.2010
Harrison, C.J.O. Bird Bones from Soldier's Hole. Accessed online at http://

www.ubss.org.uk/resources/proceedings/vol18/UBSS_Proc_18_2_258-264.pdf on 4.10.10

Huntley, J. Gates, T. & Stallibrass, S. Hadrian's Wall Research Framework: Landscape and Environment resource assessment. Accessed online at http://www.dur.ac.uk/resources/archaeological.services/research_training/hadrianswall_research_framework/project_documents/LandscapeandEnvironmentRev.pdf on 4.10.10

http://www.snh.org.uk/pdfs/scottish/ehighland/CMNNR/BlackGrouse.pdf

Bowker, Bowker and Baines 2007) featured in Southern Uplands Partnership: Black Grouse Project Report 2007, by Tom Adamson, accessed online at http://www.sup.org.uk/PDF/B-G-Final-Report.pdf on 14.6.10

Adamson, Thomas. Black Grouse Project Report for the Southern Uplands Partnership, 2007. p.12

Conserving the black grouse: 'a practical guide produced by the Game Conservancy Trust'. Accessed online at http://www.blackgrouse.info/advice/publications/BlackGrouseConservationGuide.pdf on 16.6.10

Acknowledgements

This book came about almost entirely thanks to the support of Tina Biddlecombe, who oversaw its creation with an understanding resignation.

Thanks also to Nick and Jane Smith, Colin Maxwell, Paul James, Simon Thorp, Phil Warren, John Cowan, Will Garfit, Ryan English, Jack Squires, Chris Land, Colin Blanchard and the Arran Black Grouse Group who all provided help and support in one form or another.

A special thanks to the various keepers in Scotland, England and Wales who were and continue to be instrumental to my black grouse work, but who value their privacy and the privacy of their birds more than they would a mention by name.

List of Illustrations

Index

Also published by Merlin Unwin Books

www.merlinunwin.co.uk

The Hare Jill Mason

The Otter James Williams

The Private Life of Adders Rodger McPhail

The Atlantic Salmon Malcolm Greenhalgh & Rod Sutterby

Wild Duck and their Pursuit Douglas Butler

Geese: Memoirs of a Wildfowler Edward Miller

Advice from a Gamekeeper John Cowan

The Countryman's Bedside Book BB

The Naturalist's Bedside Book BB

The Best of BB Denys Watkins Pitchford

Vintage Guns for the Modern Shot Diggory Hadoke